African Wildlife

TRiViA

Dawid van Lill

W9-DJB-936

WORLD RECORDS

Africa holds a number of world records:

- Highest sand dunes
- Largest desert
- Oldest desert
- Longest freshwater lake
- Longest river
- Largest rift valley
- Largest inland swamp
- Highest free-standing mountain
- Place experiencing most thunderstorms
- Hottest place on earth

Also, *a few near misses:*

- Second largest freshwater lake
- Second deepest freshwater lake
- Fourth largest island
- Second highest waterfall
- Second largest canyon

Some animal world records:

- Largest land mammal, with longest teeth and nose, and largest ears and legs
- Second and third largest land mammals
- Tallest land mammal, with longest tail and neck
- Largest primate
- Largest antelope
- Four of the fastest land mammals
- Largest living bird, with longest neck, legs and toes, as well as largest egg
- Fastest bird on land
- Fastest flying bird
- Bird that can dive the deepest
- Largest mammal
- Fastest fish
- Largest fish
- Largest predatory fish

More world records:

- Venomous snake with the longest teeth
- Snake responsible for the most fatal bites
- Fastest poisonous snake
- Smallest tortoise
- Largest and smallest chameleons
- Largest frog
- Largest land snail
- Noisiest insect
- Most destructive insect
- Largest, heaviest and strongest beetle
- Largest bacterium
- Bird with the largest wingspan

DID YOU KNOW?

Africa is a treasure trove of wildlife. One lifetime will not be enough to discover all the hidden wonders of this continent, and this book gives just a glimpse of the wonders that can be found on and around this continent. If the focus does sometimes wander to another continent, it will just be to compare it to Africa's wildlife. Don't worry, the main focus will remain firmly on all things African.

Enjoy the journey!

The record continent

Africa is world famous for its abundance and variety of wildlife, making it a great attraction for hundreds of thousands of visitors every year.

DID YOU KNOW?

Greenwich Mean Time (GMT) is an old concept that referred to solar time (or sun time). The term that is now used for the Greenwich time zone is Coordinated Universal Time (UTC), while Universal Time (UT) replaced the original Greenwich Mean Time.

Africa is ...

- the second largest continent
- the hottest continent
- the only continent crossed by the equator, the Tropic of Capricorn, the Tropic of Cancer and the Greenwich meridian (0° longitude)

A continent full of wildlife

- Africa has a greater variety of large ungulates (90 species) and freshwater fish (more than 2 000 species) than any other continent. It also boasts more than 1 000 mammal species and 2 300 bird species.
- Africa has 60 carnivore species, most of them natural enemies of the herbivores living on the continent.
- Among the primates are 45 baboon species, and two species of great ape – the chimpanzee and gorilla. A large number of monkeys and bushbabies live in Madagascar, which is home to most of the world's lemur species.
- A rich variety of mammals live in the oceans and seas around Africa, such as Cape fur seals, dugongs and manatees. Dolphins and whales (including toothed whales) from other parts of the world are also frequent visitors.
- Africa boasts 24% of the world's bird population (2 313 bird species from 111 families). About 1 800 species and 20 bird families are endemic to Africa, which means that they are found only in Africa.
- The islands off the African coast have huge seabird colonies and an extended range of endemic species. The Seychelles, São Tomé and Príncipe, Comoros and Mauritius all have a number of interesting and unique species, while Madagascar alone has five endemic bird families and more than 120 endemic species.
- Large birds include the ostrich, secretary bird, kori bustard (the largest flying bird), guinea fowl, pelican and flamingo. Forests are home to brightly coloured birds, such as the Knysna lourie; water birds, such as herons, storks and ibises live in Africa's large rivers and lakes, and thousands of seabirds, including the penguin, live along the continent's coasts.

Most of Africa's large variety of snakes are not venomous, but those that are may strike fear in the hearts of other creatures. Among the poisonous are the gaboon viper and other adders, cobras, mambas (black and green) and the boomslang. The python is not venomous, but constricts and suffocates its prey. Another dreaded predatory reptile is the Nile crocodile.

A very large and hot continent

Africa is the second largest of the world's seven continents, with a surface area of 30 365 000 km², or just more than 20% of the earth's total land area. It is the hottest continent, mainly because the largest part lies in the tropics, between the Tropics of Cancer and Capricorn.

DID YOU KNOW?

- East Africa has more endemic mammal species (55%), birds (63%), reptiles (49%) and amphibians (40%) than any other part of the world.
- Madagascar is the African country with the most endemic species, and ranks sixth on the world list of higher vertebrates (mammals, birds and amphibians), with more than 300 endemic species.

Variety

The animal world consists of millions of species, varying from small single-cell organisms to the giant blue whale that is as large as a school bus. Most of the animals on earth (about 85%) are insects, while only 0,3% (just more than 4 200 species) are mammals, and 0,7% (about 9 700 species) are birds.

Wow!

There are over 4 260 species of mammals on earth, as well as 6 787 species of reptiles, 9 703 species of birds and more than 28 000 fish species. The invertebrates outnumber all the vertebrates put together, with 80 000 molluscs and more than 1 million insects. Arachnids number only 44 000 species. These figures are always fluctuating because scientists keep discovering new species, while others become extinct at an alarming rate.

World records – the largest

- The African elephant is the largest **land mammal**. It is also the animal with the longest teeth and nose, and the largest ears and legs.
- The gorilla is the world's **largest primate**, and can weigh as much as 200 kg.
- The eland is the world's **largest antelope**. It can grow to a height of 2,2 m and weigh 900 kg.
- The Nile crocodile is a member of the crocodile family, and the **largest reptile** in existence. It can reach a length of up to 6 m and weigh as much as 730 kg.
- Another very large reptile is the leatherback turtle, which is about 2,4 m long and weighs an average of 540 kg.
- The African giant snail is the world's largest land gastropod. The largest known example was kept as a pet by Christopher Hudson of Hove in England. Christopher's slow-moving friend, called Gee Geronimo, was 39,37 cm long and weighed a whopping 0,907 kg.
- The longest insect in Africa is the giant stick insect that reaches lengths of 263 mm. The world's longest insect is the Borneo giant stick insect that can be as long as 328 mm (or 548 mm if the legs are stretched out).
- A bacterium from Namibia is the largest bacterium on earth. It can be 0,75 mm wide and is visible to the naked eye.

Reach for the sky, George!

The giraffe – which is about 1,8 m tall at birth – is the **tallest land mammal**, with a height of up to 5,8 m. A record-breaking giraffe, a bull named George, was sent in 1959 from Kenya to the Chester Zoo in England. The top of its horns almost touched the roof of the zoo's giraffe house, which was 6,09 m high.

Tortoise records

- The world's **smallest tortoise** is the speckled Cape tortoise (speckled padloper). Its shell has an average length of 7 cm, although some can be as short as 6 cm, while a giant speckled Cape tortoise shell can be 9,6 cm long.
- The leopard tortoise is the **second largest tortoise** in Africa and the fourth largest tortoise in the world. It can live more than 100 years.

DID YOU KNOW?

About 150 000 giant Aldabra tortoises live on the Aldabra atoll. It is the largest population of giant tortoises in the world. Adwaitya, one of the oldest known Aldabra tortoises, died in a zoo in India in March 2006. British sailors took it there in the 18th century as a gift for Lord Robert Clive of the East India Company. It was believed to be older than 250 years when it died.

More records

Madagascar, which has almost half of the world's chameleons, is home to the world's **largest AND smallest chameleons**.

- **Largest** is Parson's chameleon, which can grow to a length of 60 cm – as large as a house cat.
- **Smallest** is the pygmy leaf chameleon, which is only 35 mm long.

And more ...

- Africa's **smallest butterfly and one of the smallest in the world**, the dwarf blue or Barber's blue, is found in southern Africa. It has a maximum wingspan of about 1,2 cm.
- The emperor penguin is the bird that can **dive the deepest**. The world record is 565 m.
- Lake Malawi contains a greater variety of freshwater fish than any other lake – approximately 500 species, belonging to 10 different families.
- Lake Tanganyika is the only place where you can find large schools of freshwater sardines.
- A swan has more feathers than any other bird – more than 25 000.
- The largest seal colony in the southern hemisphere is at Cape Cross in Namibia.
- The most efficient scavenger is the spotted hyaena. It is the only animal with a digestive system that can break down bones, hoofs, horns and hides.
- The most abundant bird is a seed-eating weaver, the red-billed quelea, which has an estimated breeding population of 1,5 billion. Every year 200 million red-billed queleas are killed – and it doesn't even seem to make the slightest dent in their numbers.
- The African giant black millipede is the **world's largest millipede**. It can grow to a length of 38,7 cm, with a circumference of 6,7 cm. It has (only) 256 legs.

Not *precisely* 1 000

- There are 10 000 millipede species in the world and they have more legs than any other creature.
- 'Millipede' means '1 000 legs' and at first glance it could look as if this creature may actually have that many legs. If you should take the time to count them, you will find that it has only about 750 legs, neatly arranged in 375 pairs.
- Some millipede species have between 80 and 400 legs.
- When the millipede walks, its many feet create a wave-like motion. This is because each pair of legs is slightly out of step with the pair in front and behind.

A swarm of desert locusts, with between 40 and 80 million locusts per km², can travel from 100 to 200 kilometres a day and cover an area of 1 200 km².

What differences are there between millipedes and centipedes?

- On each segment, the millipede has two pairs of legs, while the centipede has a single pair.
- Centipedes have between 30 and 346 legs, while millipedes can have as many as 750.
- The millipede moves slower than the centipede, which is quite quick on its feet.
- Millipedes are herbivores, and centipedes are brightly coloured carnivores.

A long, long way to go

Desert locusts are the insects that migrate over the **longest distance**. In 1987 a swarm trekked in just 10 days from the west coast of Africa to the Caribbean – a trip of more than 4 500 km.

Desert locusts are normally found from Mauritania, through the Sahara Desert in northern Africa, across the Arabian Peninsula and into northwest India.

Under the right conditions, these gnawing hordes can get together and invade many countries, sweeping north as far as Spain and Russia, south to Nigeria and Kenya, and eastwards to India and southwest Asia.

Such a swarm can affect an area of 32 million km², or 20% of the world's land surface.

DID YOU KNOW?

- When the sexually undifferentiated larvae of the marine worm are exposed to females, most of them will change into dwarf males that live inside the female. In the complete absence of females, they will become females.
- This worm's skin contains a nerve poison that can paralyse small animals.

Vive la différence!

Males and females of most species differ in size, appearance and even habits, but in the case of the male marine worm, *Bonellia viridis*, it is very difficult to link it to its female counterpart.

The blue-green females can be anything from 10 to 100 cm long, while the male is a miniscule 1 to 3 mm long, and lives as a parasite inside the female.

The female of the species can thus weigh millions of times more than the male.

A massive relocation

In August 1993 the wildlife body Care for the Wild International (CFTWI) carried out the largest ever elephant relocation project.

It moved more than 500 elephants, as family groups, across Zimbabwe, from Gonarezhou National Park to the Save Valley Conservancy, a distance of 250 km. This massive operation saved these elephants from being culled.

DID YOU KNOW?

- People sometimes use the coconut crab to guard their coconut plantations.
- The adult coconut crab cannot swim, and will drown if it falls into deep water.

The name 'indri' comes from the Malagasy word 'iry', which means 'there it is'. That was what a Malagasy said when he pointed out the animal to a French naturalist, who mistook the words to be the animal's name.

A large lemur – with no tail

The **largest lemur** species is the indri or babakato, which grows to between 64 and 72 cm long. Most of this length is made up by its body and head, because it is the only lemur with almost no tail. When its arms and legs are extended, it can be as long as 120 m.

The indri is black with white patches and round ears, so it looks a little like a teddy bear.

The largest land invertebrate

The coconut crab is the **largest land invertebrate**. It has an average weight of up to 4 kg, its body is 400 mm long and its leg span is around 1 m. Some claim that it can weigh as much as 17 kg, with a body length of 1 m!

It has a pair of massive claws that it uses to lift objects as heavy as 29 kg. The claws can punch holes in a coconut through which the fruit's flesh is scooped out.

It has two powerful walking legs and can climb 6 m high into a coconut palm.

Springbok – millions and millions of them

Stories are still told of the enormous springbok herds that lived in southern Africa during the 19th century.

In 1849 John Fraser saw vast numbers of springbok (he called them 'trekbokken') passing through Beaufort West in the Karoo for a period of three days.

In 1888 a herd near Nelspoortje was believed to contain millions of springbok. Some thought there could have been 100 million, although the more realistic figure of 10 million is generally accepted.

Another herd, seen in 1896 at Karreekloof near the Orange River, covered an area 24 km wide and more than 160 km long.

A mother – many, many times over

The tenrec, one of the largest insect-eating mammals, is a prolific breeder, with the largest recorded number of young born at a single birth to a wild mammal (31 were born, of which 30 survived!). The proud mother was a tail-less tenrec, a species which is usually found in Madagascar and the Comoros Islands.

Madagascar's streaked tenrec is weaned after just five days, and within three to four weeks after birth the female of the species is ready to breed again.

The mother can feed up to 24 little tenrecs, but the normal litter size is more like 12 to 15.

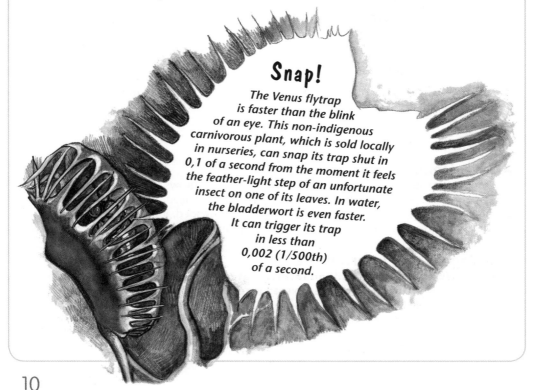

Snap!

The Venus flytrap is faster than the blink of an eye. This non-indigenous carnivorous plant, which is sold locally in nurseries, can snap its trap shut in 0,1 of a second from the moment it feels the feather-light step of an unfortunate insect on one of its leaves. In water, the bladderwort is even faster. It can trigger its trap in less than 0,002 (1/500th) of a second.

The largest leaves

The raffia palm has enormous leaves. One leaf can be as long as 25 m and 3 m wide, while its stalk could be a further 4 m long.

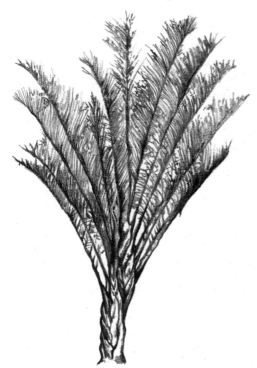

DID YOU KNOW?

♦ After its bark has been cut, the raffia palm's sap, a milky white liquid, is traditionally collected in a large gourd. Because the bark has been deeply cut, the tree will die.

♦ The sap is allowed to ferment for a few days and then drunk as wine – or distilled into stronger liquor.

♦ Castor bean seeds have been found in Egyptian tombs dating back to 4000 BC, and in their day writers like Herodotus were aware of the use of castor seed oil for lighting and body anointment.

♦ The name **Ricinus** is Latin for 'tick': castor bean seeds are so named because their form resembles that of certain ticks.

The deadliest bean

The castor oil plant is a member of the Euphorbia family and the only member of the genus *Ricinus*. Its seed, the castor bean (not a true bean), is the source of castor oil which has been known to bring a grimace to many a child's face.

Raw castor beans contain ricin, a deadly poison, which makes the castor bean the most poisonous plant known to humans.

Ricin, which even in very small amounts is lethal, is 6 000 times more poisonous than cyanide and 12 000 times more poisonous than rattlesnake venom.

One of the deadliest diseases?

Rabies encephalitis is a feared viral infection of the central nervous system, and nearly always proves fatal.

A rabid animal's bite is not always a death sentence, however. Immediate treatment can prevent the virus from entering the central nervous system, thus improving the victim's chance of survival.

The largest flyer — ever?

About 70 million years ago, in North America and Africa, the largest flying creature that ever lived terrorized other animals from the air. It was a pterosaur called *Quetzalcoatlus northropi* ('feathered serpent') that weighed about 86 kg and had a wingspan of 11 m.

DID YOU KNOW?

- *The aardvark has a long, narrow head with a pig-like snout.*
- *It has very long ears, like those of a rabbit, which can move independently of each other.*
- *Despite its name and appearance, it is not family of the pig or the rabbit.*
- *The aardvark has white hairs, 2,5 to 5 cm long, that grow from its nostrils. When it digs, these hairs and skin-folds cover the nostrils to protect its nose from dirt and insects.*

Curiouser and curiouser

The aardvark ('earth pig') is such a peculiar animal that it cannot be classified in a family with any other living mammal species. It is placed all on its own in an order of mammals known as the *Tubulidentata* ('tube-toothed').

Its 20 teeth, near the back of its jaws, never stop growing. A tooth has no root or enamel, but a fine tube that runs through it – that is why it has been named 'tube-toothed'.

Its thin, sticky tongue is 45 cm long and perfect for slipping down holes of termite nests to lap up insects.

The short, powerful legs, each with four webbed toes, end in long blunt claws that are stronger than the head of a pick-axe.

The lone wolf

The world's rarest species of wild dog is the Ethiopian wolf, which is also the rarest carnivore species in Africa, with fewer than 40 wolves remaining.

So thick-skinned ...

- Some large mammals, such as the elephant, hippopotamus and rhinoceros, are called 'pachyderms', a word which means 'thick skin'.
- The rhinoceros has the thickest skin of any land mammal, and the thickest skin in relation to its size. The skin on its back and sides can average 2,5 cm.
- The elephant's skin is also very thick, varying in places from 2 to 3 cm.

A very long guest

- The pork tapeworm is an unwelcome guest that makes itself at home in the human intestines, sometimes reaching lengths of more than 6 m.
- The beef tapeworm can be even more invasive – it will grow to lengths of more than 15 m.
- The fish tapeworm can be found in the small intestines of fish and humans. It has an average length of between 9 and 12 m, but some large specimens have grown to double that size, occupying a full 18 m of its host's intestines.

Don't let the bedbugs bite!

We may share our beds with common bedbugs, parasites that like to take a sip of our blood now and then. They are not greedy, however, and can easily go without feeding for more than a year.

'That's nothing!', the soft tick will brag. This little eight-legged horror, whose bite can spread a bacterium that causes fever, can stay without food for up to five years.

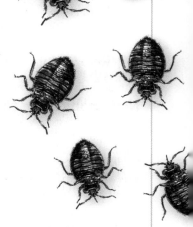

Not welcome!

Another unwelcome – and uninvited – intestinal guest is the roundworm, which is believed to have made itself at home in more than 1 billion people all over the world.

To add insult to injury, the female can produce 200 000 eggs a day – that's every day of her adult life!

She can produce a total of 26 million eggs in her lifetime, and these eggs can survive in almost any conditions.

Chromosome records

- Each body cell's nucleus contains a number of chromosomes, arranged in pairs. These chromosomes are rod-shaped structures, carrying the genes that determine the gender and certain characteristics that an organism inherits from its parents.
- A normal human body cell has 46 chromosomes, arranged in 23 pairs.
- The organism with the highest number of chromosomes yet recorded is the adder's tongue fern, with 720 pairs.
- The roundworm is at the other end of the scale, with only one set of chromosomes. Close contenders are the mosquito (three sets), and the fruit fly (a meagre four sets).
- Most birds have more chromosomes than humans. The canary, duck and rock pigeon have 80, the chicken 78 and house sparrow 76.
- Mammals with more chromosomes than humans include cattle (60), horses and guinea pigs (64), and dogs (78).
- Mammals with fewer chromosomes include the mole (34), cat and pig (38), and rat (42). The kangaroo has only 22 chromosomes.

Family of man

- The oldest non-human primate was a chimpanzee named Gamma, who died at the age of 59 years and five months in Atlanta, Georgia.
- Madagascar's pygmy mouse lemur, which weighs just 30,6 g, is the world's smallest primate. The total length of its head and body is 6,1 cm, with its tail adding a further 13,7 cm.
- The eastern lowland gorilla of the eastern DRC and southwestern Uganda stands 1,75 m tall and weighs an impressive 165 kg, more than any Springbok forward in the history of South African rugby.
- The mountain gorilla, which lives in western Rwanda, southwestern Uganda and the eastern DRC, is almost as large as the eastern lowland gorilla, with an average height of 1,73 m and weight of about 155 kg.
- A 1,88 m mountain gorilla, shot in the eastern DRC in 1920, is the tallest recorded wild gorilla. Colossus, an eastern lowland male, was the tallest gorilla in captivity. It was also about 1,88 m tall, but weighed a massive 260,8 kg. It must have looked like a sumo wrestler!

New monkey on the block

In 2003 the first new African monkey to have been discovered for over 20 years was found. Two separate teams, working in Tanzania, came upon this 90 cm long, brownish monkey, known to locals as 'kipunji'.

With its black face and paws, long tail and off-white belly, scientists soon realized that it was a mangabey monkey. Its crest and bushy whiskers gave its head a triangular shape, and it had a very unusual low-pitched, honking bark-like cry, quite unlike other mangabeys.

The scorpion king

At lengths of more than over 20 cm, southern Africa's long-tailed scorpion is probably the longest in the world.

It's a slo-o-ow grower

The animal kingdom's slowest-growing organism is the deep-sea clam, which reaches a length of 8 mm in (just!) 100 years.

A nearly invisible snake

The thread snake and brahminy blindsnake both grow to a maximum length of 10,8 cm, making them the shortest snakes in the world. The brahminy blindsnake is only about 0,16 cm broad. It is drab-coloured and reclusive, and can usually be found in soil or rotting plant material.

Short but deadly

The shortest venomous snake is Namibia's Namaqua or spotted dwarf adder, with an average length of 200 mm.

From bad to worse

The great white shark is the world's biggest meat-eating shark. Yet it is much smaller than the Megalodon, the largest meat-eating shark that ever lived. This giant, which grew to be as long as 12 m, lived between 25 million and 1,6 million years ago. Each of its teeth was the size of a human hand.

> ### DID YOU KNOW?
> The ocean around the Seychelles islands is home to the whale shark, the world's largest fish.

Seeing double

The Seychelles in the Indian Ocean is where the double coconut or coco-de-mer thrives. The name means 'coconut of the sea' and it is the single-seeded fruit of the giant fan palm, the largest seed of all plants.

It is 30 cm long, with a circumference of 0,9 m, and can weigh as much as 20 kg. It is found in the wild only on the Seychelles.

Largest lily leaves

The botanical gardens of Mauritius are famous for their collection of giant Amazon water lilies. Its leaves are more than 2 m in diameter and its stems are as long as 6 m.

A leaf may cover about the same area as a small trampoline and is strong enough for a child to sit on it.

Pink pigeons – and a few falcons

The pink pigeon is found in the southwestern corner of Mauritius and, while its numbers dropped to 15 or 20 in 1985, still only 250 birds remain today.

The world's rarest falcon lives on Mauritius, too. By the 1970s the Mauritius kestrel's population was reduced to four, but an intensive breeding programme has since increased the population to more than 350.

Old four-legs

The coelacanth, a prehistoric fish dating back 400 million years and once thought to be extinct, is still found in the sea around the Comoros Islands. The first specimen was found in 1938 in Chalumna Bay near East London and identified by Professor JLB Smith. Since then, live coelacanths have been captured from time to time, and many have been filmed in their natural habitat. Its four lobed fins led to its nickname, 'old four-legs'.

Gentle giant

The African elephant is huge – the largest living land mammal. This giant is 6,4 m long, nearly 4 m tall and weighs as much as 6 tons. How does this compare to, say, an ordinary man, weighing 80 kg and standing 1,80 m in his shoes?

Well, as the man weighs 80 kg, it would take 75 men of his size to be on equal terms with one elephant. If he stands on the shoulders of another equally tall man, they would still be 40 cm smaller than the elephant.

It's not a good idea to try running away from a charging elephant, even if you are a speedster. It may look as if this giant is just ambling along, but when it gets angry enough to charge, it reaches speeds of between 30 and 40 km/h. When Asafa Powell, the human world record holder for sprinting over a distance of 100 m, set his record time of 9,77 seconds, he was charging along the track at a speed of (only) slightly faster than 36 km/h.

Somewhat smaller

At the other end of the scale is the smallest mammal in Africa – the shrew. Every member of this family is an itty-bitty jittery little thing, with the smallest – the rare Gabon shrew – weighing in at less than 10 g. It would take 600 000 shrews to actually balance a (large) pair of scales if they were on one side and an elephant on the other side. Just one of the four huge teeth in an elephant's mouth weighs as much as 400 of these shrews.

Massive molars

How many teeth does an elephant have? We usually see only the two large ivory tusks, which have been known to reach a record length of 3,84 m, but the elephant is the proud owner of 24 other teeth, of which only four will be in its mouth at a time. The four teeth inside an elephant's mouth are enormous – 30 cm long and 10 cm wide – and each weighs 4 kg.

As soon as one set of four teeth has been worn away, these teeth fall out, and are replaced by the next set of four. The last set to appear will have the largest teeth, which can be as long as 40 cm and weigh 5 kg.

DID YOU KNOW?

- The largest elephant recorded was shot in Mucusso, Angola, in 1974. Its height was estimated to be 3,96 m, and its length, from trunk to tail, was 10,6 m. Its weight was estimated at 12,24 tons and its forefoot had a circumference of 1,8 m.
- Damaraland in Namibia produces the tallest African elephants, members of an endangered desert species. The tallest specimen was a bull killed in 1978 near Sesfontein. Its standing height was estimated to be about 4,21 m and it was 10,38 m long. Its forefoot circumference was 1,57 m. And its weight? A whopping eight tons!

The tusks

The elephant's tusks consist of ivory, which is a fine-grained, opaque, creamy white, hard dentine that forms in layers.

Elephant ivory is unique and consists of fine criss-cross lines in a diamond pattern that is clearly visible in the cross-section of a tusk.

Elephants are left-tusked or right-tusked, because every elephant uses one tusk more than the other, causing the most-used tusk to wear down quicker than the other.

Depending on the temperature, an elephant drinks between 100 and 300 litres of water per day, and daily produces about 110 kg of dung as well as 50 litres of urine.

DID YOU KNOW?

An elephant chews by moving its jaws backwards and forwards – unlike cattle that move their jaws from side to side.

Leviathan of the deep

But wait! Even the elephant's impressive size pales to insignificance when it is compared to the enormous blue whale. As far as we know, this leviathan of the deep is the largest animal that ever lived.

A blue whale cow that was caught in 1926 was 33,27 m long, and weighed 190 tons – as much as 32 large elephants.

The blue whale's tongue alone is as large as an elephant, and its heart is as big as a Volkswagen Beetle. Compared to this great size, the elephant's heart is quite small, weighing between 20 and 30 kg.

DID YOU KNOW?

The blue whale's scientific name is **Balaenoptera musculus**. Balaenoptera *means 'winged whale' and* musculus *is a Latin word meaning 'little mouse'.*

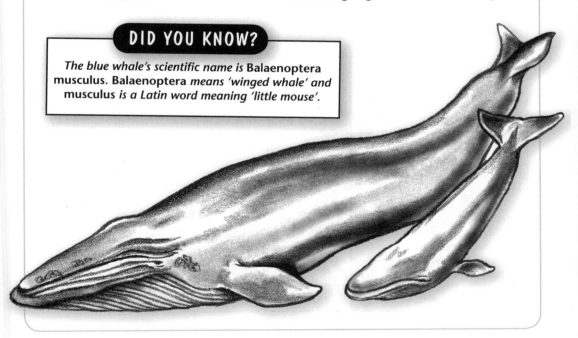

Sounding off

The blue whale is quite raucous. It uses low-frequency pulses to communicate with other whales, and these pulses have been measured at volumes of up to 188 decibels – the loudest sound emitted by any living being. A passenger jet taking off generates about 120 decibels.

The blue whale's sounds have been detected as far away as 850 km.

HOW ANIMALS SOUND

People are always trying to find ways of describing animal noises. Some of these names are nothing less than an imitation of the sound, while others do not seem to have any relation to the sound itself.

Apes gibber	**Hyaenas** laugh
Bees hum and buzz	**Lions** roar
Beetles drone	**Mice** squeak and squeal
Bitterns boom	**Monkeys** gibber
Chaffinches fink	**Nightingales** pipe and warble
Crows caw	**Owls** screech, shriek and hoot
Cuckoos cuckoo	**Parrots** talk
Dolphins click	**Pigeons** coo
Doves coo	**Snakes** hiss
Eagles scream	**Sparrows** chirp
Elephants trumpet	**Swallows** twitter
Falcons chant	**Swans** cry
Foxes bark and yelp	**Thrushes** whistle
Frogs croak	**Vultures** scream
Giraffes bleat	**Walruses** ort
Grasshoppers chirp	**Whales** sing
Hares squeak or scream	**Wolves** howl

DID YOU KNOW?

- Cats can make over 100 individual vocal sounds, but dogs can only manage 10.
- The Basenji of central Africa is the only dog that does not bark.
- Hippopotamuses make 80% of their sounds under water.
- Only full-grown male crickets can chirp.
- Cheetahs make a noise that sounds like a bird's chirp, and can be heard as far away as 1,6 km.

Unexpected sounds

- The snapping shrimp is only 3,8 cm long, but it can use its big claw to create a snapping sound exactly like that of a firecracker.
- The Madagascar hissing cockroach creates its sound by expelling air through the spiracles on its abdomen. The courtship hiss differs enough from the hiss a male uses to establish his territory, leaving no doubt about his meaning.
- The African penguin is known by a more common name: jackass penguin. That's because it can utter a braying sound that sounds just like the call of your local farmyard donkey.
- The eland, Africa's largest antelope, can't rely on stealth to get around unnoticed, because its knees make a loud clicking sound when it walks. This is a dead giveaway – sometimes taken quite literally by a hungry predator.

Shrill and very loud

The noisiest insect is the cicada, which produces a 'song' with an intensity of 106,7 decibels (about the same volume as a power saw) at a distance of 50 cm.

The male is the one with the loud voice, which is produced by drum-like membranes, called 'tymbals'. These tymbals are part of the exoskeleton and are modified to form rapidly vibrating membranes that cause the well-known sound.

The cicada's repertoire consists of three songs. The first is to chat with other cicadas, the second is a serenade for its courting trips, and the last one is a special emergency sound for all those times when it feels threatened.

DID YOU KNOW?

- An adult cicada is sometimes called an 'imagine'.
- Adult cicadas are between 2 and 5 cm long, but some tropical species can be as long as 15 cm.
- Desert cicadas can cool themselves by sweating, especially when the air temperature rises above 39°C.

The king has spoken

- When a lion roars it can literally make the dust fly.
- The lion's roar is produced by a special two-plate hyoid or tongue bone in its throat. (All cat species that cannot roar have only one hyoid.)
- A lion's roar can boom over the plains at 114 decibels and can be heard at a distance of up to 8 km.
- Males start roaring when they are one year old and females start soon after that. The male's roar sounds deeper and louder than that of the female.
- A lion normally stands when it roars, and it can roar at any time and anywhere – it is, after all, king of the beasts!

A lion's claws

- The lion has five toes on its front paws and four on each hind paw. It literally walks on its toes.
- The fifth toe ('thumb') of the front paw sits higher than the other toes and slightly behind them and it does not show in a lion's tracks.
- The lion's nails are very strong and they stay sharp because they can be retracted. A nail grows in layers, and when an old layer is worn away, it falls off and a new layer grows out.
- One of the lethal nails can be 38 mm long from paw to point.

DID YOU KNOW?

- The lion is the largest African carnivore. The average African lion is about 2,7 m long, 91 to 97 cm high at the shoulder, and weighs anywhere between 181 and 185 kg.
- The heaviest wild specimen was shot near Hectorspruit in South Africa in 1936. It weighed 313 kg.
- Simba, a black-maned lion at Colchester Zoo in Essex, England, weighed 375 kg and had a shoulder height of 1,11 m.

DID YOU KNOW?

- The lion often uses its thumb talon or 'false toe' on his front paw as a toothpick!
- The black tuft of hair at the tip of the tail hides a sharp talon (almost like a nail), consisting of the last five tail-bones which are fused.
- The lion is the only big cat with tufts of hair on its 'elbows'.

Hearing it all

- Cats have a hearing range of between 100 and 60 000 Hz.
- A dog hears sounds with a frequency as high as 40 000 Hz.
- A pigeon can detect sounds as low as 0,1 Hz.
- The elephant has a hearing range of between 1 and 20 000 Hz. The very low frequency sounds are in the infrasound range. Humans cannot hear sounds in this range.
- A rat's hearing range is between 1 000 and 90 000 Hz.
- A dolphin can hear frequencies of up to at least 100 000 Hz.
- Grasshoppers can hear frequencies of up to 50 000 Hz.
- Bats are able to hear frequencies between 3 000 and 120 000 Hz.
- Mice can hear frequencies of between 1 000 and 100 000 Hz.
- Humans hear frequencies between 20 and 20 000 Hz.
- The noctuid moth has a hearing range of between 1 000 and 240 000 Hz.

CAN YOU BELIEVE IT?

- ◆ A cat's ear contains 32 muscles. The cat can rotate each ear rapidly to identify sounds, and its hearing is acute enough to hear the ultrasonic sounds made by rodents. Cats can hear 10 octaves, while humans hear only 8,5 octaves.
- ◆ A dog swivels its ears to locate the source of a sound in 6/100ths of a second. It can hear sounds that are 230 m away, while humans would only hear similar sounds at a distance of 23 m.
- ◆ Zebras can rotate their ears to detect sounds – without moving their bodies.
- ◆ Most mammals lose the hair inside their ears as they get older – something which can contribute to hearing loss. Bats, however, are an exception to this rule for they can regenerate the cells within their ears and grow new hair.

More ear facts

- The cricket 'hears' with its legs – sound waves cause vibrations in a thin membrane on the cricket's front legs.
- Tarantulas and other spiders sense vibrations through hairs on their legs.
- Ants can 'hear' with their knees, picking up vibrations both in their nests and when they are on the ground.
- A frog has an eardrum or tympanic membrane on the outside of its body, just behind its eye.
- Snakes have no external ears so they cannot hear as we do. However, sound waves may travel through bones in their heads to the inner ear.

Ear! Ear!

The fennec is the smallest of all foxes, but it has the largest ears. Its head and body may only measure between 35 and 41 cm, but its ears are 15 cm long. As there is little water in a desert – the habitat of fennecs – they do not sweat to keep cool. They have a high skin temperature, so that heat flows from their bodies, except when the air temperature is very high. Their big ears are probably an advantage, because a lot of body heat can be lost to the air through their large surface areas.

The elephant's ears

Temperatures on the African plains can sometimes climb quite high, so African elephants use their huge ears to keep cool. Flapping their ears helps the elephant to get rid of heat through blood vessels that lie just under the surface of the skin. The ears' large surface area causes blood to move faster, helping the animal to cool down.

As each elephant's ears look different, individuals can be identified by their ears. Identifying features to look for are the size of the ears, the tears and indents in them, and their network of blood vessels.

Collective names for animals

People have always been fascinated by groups of animals, possibly because they feel that one group of animals just has to be distinguished from another. That could be why there are such creative names to describe groups of animals.

- A shrewdness of apes
- A cete of badgers
- A sounder of warthogs
- A pod of dolphins
- A skulk of foxes

- A pride of lions
- A pod of seals
- A gam, herd, pod or school of whales
- A pack or rout of wolves

The heart – relatively speaking

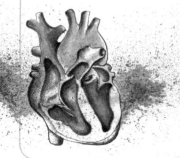

The sizes of animal hearts differ enormously – from the whale's heart, which is as large as a small car, to the shrew's tiny, tiny heart, which weighs only 0,11 g.

What is interesting, though, is to look at the weight of the heart relative to an animal's body weight. A human heart, for example, weighs 4,3% of a person's body weight. On this scale an electric ray's heart weighs only 0,6% of its body weight, while the hummingbird's tiny heart (0,09 g) accounts for a massive 23,9% of its body weight!

The relative heart weights for the crocodile (2,6%), the python (3%), the lion (3%) and the bullfrog (3,1%) are about the same, just below that of the sperm whale (3,2%). The African elephant has a slightly higher ratio (3,9%), while the rhinoceros (6,3%) and the common house mouse (6,45%) are quite similar. The tiny shrew's relative heart weight is 14%.

Most of the higher relative heart weights belong to birds, with the ostrich recording 9,8%, domestic pigeon 14%, swallow 14,1%, house sparrow 15,2%, European starling 16,2% and the common swift 16,5%.

Hearts aflutter

An elephant's heart beats between 22 and 28 times per minute when it is resting, while the human's average heart rate is 72 beats per minute.

Compared to this, the shrew's tiny heart fairly races along. When the shrew is calm and collected, its heart will beat only 660 times per minute; when it is agitated, it can go up to 1 200 beats per minute, and in one case it was measured at 1 511 beats per minute!

And the blue whale's resting heart rate? Only 5 to 10 beats per minute.

HEART RATES OF ANIMALS (IN BEATS PER MINUTE)

Species – Vertebrates	Heartbeats	Species – Vertebrates	Heartbeats	Species – Invertebrates	Heartbeats
Shrew	500–1 320	Human	60–90	Fruit fly	235
Sparrow	745–850	Sheep	60–80	Woodlouse	180–200
Swift	700	Ostrich	60–70	Shrimp	146
Bat	660	Dog	60–180	Anopheles mosquito	110
Mouse	450–550	Cattle	45–50		
Crow	380	Carp	40–80	Migratory locust	80–130
Chicken	330–375	Common toad	40–50		
Hedgehog (not hibernating)	280–320	Lion	40	Cockroach	60–80
		Goldfish	36–40	Dragonfly	60
Brown rat	260–450	Common frog	35–40	Edible snail	40–50
Duck	229–420	Horse	32–44	Lobster	50
Rabbit	150–280	Giant tortoise	30–40	Octopus	33–40
Goose	110–130	Elephant	22–28	Butterfly	29
Fox	100	Hedgehog	18	Stag beetle	16
Cat	80	Electric ray	16–50		
Giraffe	66	Whale	15–16		
Pig	60–80	Eel	10–15		

THE HARD-WORKING HEART

How hard does a heart work? Here is an indication of the amount of work certain mammals' hearts have to do in a lifetime.

Mammal	Weight (Kg)	Heart rate (Beats/min)	Longevity (Years)	Lifetime beats (Billions)
Human	90	60	70	2,21
Chicken	1,5	275	15	2,17
Monkey	5	190	15	1,5
Cat	2	150	15	1,18
Elephant	5 000	30	70	1,1
Rabbit	1	205	9	0,97
Horse	1 200	44	40	0,93
Pig	150	70	25	0,92
Large whale	120 000	20	80	0,84
Cow	800	65	22	0,75
Medium dog	50	90	15	0,71
Hamster	0,06	450	3	0,71
Giraffe	900	65	20	0,68
Large dog	8	75	17	0,67
Small dog	2	100	10	0,53

The heart is the snitch!

Sharks use ampullae of Lorenzini to sense small electrochemical impulses that are sent from the bodies of animals when they move.

Even when prey is motionless, it cannot escape detection by the shark's ampullae because its heart – which is a muscle – is still moving, giving the shark a constant supply of information.

The ampullae are placed on the snout of the shark, and contain many small jelly-filled tubules with small cells that are very sensitive to electrochemical impulses.

CAN YOU BELIEVE IT?

- An octopus has three hearts, an earthworm has five hearts and worms have up to 10 hearts.
- A human heart beats about 100 000 times per day.
- Little brown bats can reduce their heart rate to 20 beats per minute and can stop breathing altogether for 48 minutes at a time while hibernating. If they are not disturbed, they may hibernate for more than seven months. If they wake up too many times in a winter, they will run out of energy reserves and die before spring arrives.
- Nile crocodiles have four-chambered hearts, just like birds and humans, but because they are cold-blooded they still rely on the sun for heat.
- The giraffe has the highest blood pressure of any animal. Its heart is large (it weighs nearly 12 kg) and can pump 606 litres of blood per minute.
- An anticoagulant made from vampire bat saliva could soon be used to treat human heart patients and stroke victims.

A long way to the top

The giraffe's heart, which is 0,6 m long and weighs about 12 kg, beats an average of 65 times a minute. The walls of this big heart are 7,5 cm thick and must be very strong to pump blood to the head and brain – against the earth's gravity.

The giraffe's blood pressure is two to three times that of humans. The upper part of the neck has a network of specialized arteries that controls blood pressure and ensures the brain always has the correct quantity of blood when the animal lifts or lowers its head. The neck arteries have specially adapted valves that help to control the blood flow and blood pressure.

The blood pressure in the legs is very high – that is why the skin is thick and very tight around the legs. It works almost like the suits worn by astronauts.

A spider has transparent blood. A mammal's blood is red, an insect has yellow blood and a lobster's blood is blue.

Bulky baobabs

Just when you thought, 'Wow! The blue whale is humongous!', along comes the baobab tree. In the Limpopo Province, near Tzaneen, is a 6 000-year-old specimen of this tree, also known as the 'upside down tree', which is 22 m tall and has a girth of 47 m. The trunk has been hollowed out and a small pub has been built inside, complete with seats, a music system and space for 60 people.

Baobab facts

- A 'normal' baobab with a circumference of about 30 m can store nearly 100 000 litres of water, which weighs about 100 tons.
- The baobab is an important food source for local elephants, monkeys and baboons, and one of its fruits has the same vitamin C content as four oranges.
- The flowers are pollinated by bats and bushbabies, and the pollen can be used as glue.
- The seeds are a source of protein, oil and phosphates; they also have a high calcium content.
- Even the trunk is useful – because it is fibrous, it can be woven into rope mats and paper.
- And the bark? You can use it to make beer and tea.

Lazy lions

Under a shady tree. That's where you will most probably find the nearest lion, which may look quite regal, but is in fact a lazy layabout. During the day it prefers resting in the shade of a tree, especially after a meal. The male leaves the task of hunting to female members of the pride, even though they have a rather poor success rate (between 15 and 20%). When they do succeed in killing prey, the male will suddenly find enough energy to amble over to the kill and gorge itself, gobbling up between 20 and 30 kg of meat. Afterwards it will be at its laziest, sleeping for as long as 24 hours.

Sleepyhead! Or not …

Some animals sleep a lot; others don't need much sleep at all. An elephant needs only three hours of sleep a day, while the mighty lion will regularly sleep as long as 12 hours, and a cat could easily snooze for 15 hours.

That's fortunate for the tiny mouse, which will sleep only three hours a day, keeping one eye open anyway. Just in case …

ANIMALS: DAILY SLEEP REQUIRED

Animal	Hours	Animal	Hours
Donkey	3	African pouched rat	8
Horse	3	Pig	8
Zebra	3	Shrew	9
Cow	4	Chimpanzee	10
Giraffe	2–4	Baboon	10
Sheep	4	Rabbit	11
Goat	4	Gorilla	12
Tree hyrax	5	Mouse	13
Genet	6	Tenrec	13
Human	7	Cat	15

The tallest of them all

- Taller than 268 baobab trees or 1 473 elephants is Mount Kilimanjaro, a currently dormant but active volcano near the equator.
- Kilimanjaro is the tallest of all Africa's mountains, the highest free-standing mountain in the world and the highest mountain on or near the equator.
- The central peak, Kibo, is the highest of its three volcanic peaks – 5 892 m above sea level – and is connected by a broad saddle to another peak, Mawenzi, which is 5 149 m high.
- The height of Kibo was initially recorded as 5 895 m, but scientists using the more accurate global positioning system (GPS) have since found that the correct height is 'only' 5 892 m.

Higher and higher

Kilimanjaro is 5 892 m high, nearly 3 km lower than the world's highest mountain, Mount Everest, which lies on the border between Nepal and Tibet and is 8 850 m above sea level.

If a mountain's height is measured from its base under the sea to its peak, Mauna Kea on Hawaii is actually the world's highest mountain at 10 203 m, although only 4 245 m is above sea level.

To put everything in perspective, remember that the highest mountain in our solar system is Olympus Mons on Mars. It is about 26 000 m high, three times as high as Everest.

CAN YOU BELIEVE IT?

- *In spite of its location near the equator, Kilimanjaro's top is always covered in snow and ice. This feature has been immortalized in print by Ernest Hemingway who wrote about this majestic mountain in his classic* The Snows of Kilimanjaro *(1936).*
- *Research indicates that 33% of Kilimanjaro's snow and ice has disappeared over the past two decades, and it now has 82% less ice than in 1912.*
- *The name 'Kilimanjaro' is said to mean 'mountain of the god of cold', and comes from the Swahili* kilima *(mountain) and* njaro *(god of cold).*

AFRICA'S HIGHEST MOUNTAINS

No.	Mountain	Highest point	Height	Country
1	Mount Kilimanjaro	Kibo-Uhuru Peak	5 892 m	Tanzania
2	Mount Kenya	Nelion Peak	5 199 m	Kenya
3	Mawensi	Hans Meyer Peak	5 149 m	Tanzania
4	Mount Stanley	Margherita Peak	5 109 m	DRC/Uganda
5	Mount Speke	Vittorio Emanuele Peak	4 890 m	Uganda
6	Mount Baker	Edward Peak	4 844 m	Uganda
7	Mount Emin	Umberto Peak	4 798 m	DRC
8	Mount Gessi	Iolanda Peak	4 715 m	Uganda
9	Mount Luigi di Savoia	Sella Peak	4 627 m	Uganda
10	Ras Dashen Terara	Ras Dashen Terara (Ancua)	4 620 m	Ethiopia

A slow grower

An oak tree can grow very old – reaching more than 900 years – and a mature oak tree needs as much as 90 litres of water per day. These giants are very slow growers, gaining only about 1,4 mm per day or 0,5 m per year.

Lichens grow even more slowly – only about 0,0025 mm per day.

The fast grower

The eucalyptus tree, which has been introduced to Africa from Australia, is the continent's fastest growing tree. It can shoot up at a tempo of 2,5 cm per day or more than 9 m in a year.

From egg to adult

A crocodile egg is about 8 cm long, and when it hatches, the little crocodile is about 26 cm long. It grows to an impressive adult length of more than 5 m. The golden eagle, which also lays eggs 8 cm long, fortunately does not share the crocodile's growth pattern. The eagle is just 13 cm long when it hatches, and grows only to a height of 88 cm – measured from beak to tail.

DID YOU KNOW?

If a 50 cm human baby should copy the Nile crocodile's growth pattern, it would eventually shoot up to become a 9,5 m adult.

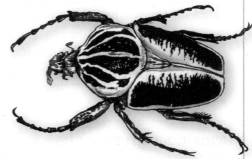

A true goliath

The goliath beetle, 11 cm long and weighing 100 g, is the world's heaviest flying beetle. By comparison, the house mouse has a body that is 6,5 cm long and weighs just 12 g.

How strong are you?

- It does not seem as if a weight-lifting contest between a human and an ant is fair, but size for size, it is actually no contest at all. The ant will win hands down, because it can lift and carry up to 50 times its own body weight. If an 80 kg man could achieve this, he would be able to lift (and carry) 4 000 kg or three family cars.
- A gorilla is eight times stronger than a human, and would be able to lift two tons.
- An elephant can carry only 25% of its own weight on its back, while a camel can transport 20% of its body weight. A really strong person is able to pick up objects three times his/her own weight.
- The world's weight-lifting champion is the rhinoceros beetle, an impressive insect that can grow to a length of 45 cm. It can easily be regarded as the world's strongest living creature, because according to some sources it can carry 850 times its own weight!

Excellent cuisine – naturally!

The hidden menu

Humans eat more than 500 kinds of insects – voluntarily. Microscopic parts of another 900 insect species are literally 'hidden' in the flour we use for our daily bread, in the chocolate that satisfies our sweet tooth, in the vegetables that are good for us and in the fruit we enjoy. Such insect parts also lurk in tomato sauce, peanut butter and canned sweetcorn.

Don't worry! Health authorities have strict guidelines for the acceptable levels of insect parts in food. The chemicals necessary to eliminate these insect parts completely would cause a more serious threat to people than the insect parts.

Tasty termites

Fried termites, without their wings, are a delicacy and a good source of protein in some parts of Africa. On the shores of Lake Victoria the local people have decided to turn a major source of irritation – the clouds of midges that hover overhead – into a source of sustenance. They catch handfuls of the tiny insects and press them into cakes that are baked and enjoyed. Problem solved!

Pan-fried weevils

The palm weevil of Nigeria is a large insect with fat, fleshy larvae. A tip: when the larvae are pan fried they make a delicious snack, just like South Africa's mopane worm (which is actually the emperor moth in disguise). These fat, juicy grubs can even be bought at the local supermarket, and are commonly sold as dried snacks.

Nutritious grub(s)

A smallish grasshopper is an excellent source of protein (20,6 g per 100 g) and fat (6,1 g per 100 g), while a dung beetle is only slightly less nutritious. It contains less protein (17,2 g protein per 100 g), but more fat (8,3 g of fat per 100 g). By the way, 100 g of ground beef will give you 27,4 g of protein and 21,2 g of fat.

CAN YOU BELIEVE IT?

- Jerboas can reach speeds of up to 25 km/h when they are chased by predators. They bound from side to side in a zigzag pattern to help confuse their numerous enemies.
- A jerboa has different types of burrows. Temporary burrows are not very long. Another type of burrow, used for escape from predators during the night, is unsealed and not camouflaged. The temporary daytime burrow is camouflaged and sealed.
- Permanent burrows, which have several entrances, are sealed and camouflaged, and may have a nesting chamber, food storage chambers and a hibernation chamber between 1,5 and 2,5 m below the surface.

Jumping for survival?

The jerboa is a small jumping rodent that is well adapted to life in the desert. It has short front legs and long hind legs, and a long tail with a tuft at the end. When it is sitting, it uses the tail as a prop.

The jerboa is an excellent jumper. It can cover 2,5 m in a single leap. By hopping to move around, the animal conserves energy, and by burrowing it is able to escape from the effects of extreme heat or cold.

DID YOU KNOW?

Jerboas are highly successful desert animals. They can live in both hot and cold deserts and survive without having to drink water – though they do have some creative ways to get moisture. They save the moisture in their breath by sleeping in underground burrows with their bushy tails over their mouths.

When food is scarce a jerboa will eat its own dung – for moisture and vitamins.

Jump for joy!

◆ In 1910, MB Mitzman did a series of experiments and discovered that a 1,5 mm human flea can jump an amazing 33 cm – 220 times its body length. If a 1,75 m tall male athlete could achieve this feat, the world record for the long jump would be 385 m, instead of the current 8,95 m.

◆ The world record of 8,95 m, held by Mike Powell, is quite good compared to those of other mammals. It is nearly five times his body length.

◆ The impala can jump a distance of 10 m (six times its body length).

◆ Compared to this, the lion is an average jumper. It can achieve a distance of only 4 to 5 m, which is between two and three times its body length.

DID YOU KNOW?

◆ The goliath frog is 30 cm long and can leap 3 m – 10 times its body length.

◆ The sharp-nosed ridged frog can jump 3,6 m, or 45 times its body length.

◆ A grasshopper can jump 2 m, about 33 times its body length, while the mammal with the most spring in its step is the jerboa. Its long hind legs enable it to leap a distance of 2,5 m (15 times its body length).

The killing machine

The innocent-looking ladybird is in fact a dangerous killing machine in disguise. It can devour up to 50 aphids per day, which means it will notch up an impressive 5 000 victims in its short life.

◆ And how does the ladybird prevent other predators from snacking on it? It leaks chemicals from its knee joints – nasty, foul-tasting stuff, which will put off even those with the most undiscerning palates.

◆ If all else fails, the ladybird's bright red colour scheme seems to scream: 'Don't eat me! Don't even consider it!' It seems to work quite well.

All *about tongues*

- Animal tongues come in all shapes and sizes, which make them one of the more interesting body parts.
- The blue whale has the largest tongue of any animal. It is about 5,5 m long and weighs between 5 and 8 tons – as much as an adult elephant. In fact, this tongue is so large that 50 people could easily stand on it. Compared to this record, any other animal's tongue pales to insignificance.
- There are other animals with impressive tongues, however. The giraffe's spectacular blue-black tongue can be 50 cm long and is covered with sticky saliva. The long-neck uses its tongue to clean its eyes – and even its ears, if it should feel like it. The wicked-looking thorns of its favourite thorn trees do not worry the giraffe, because it can easily manoeuvre its tongue past them and the thick saliva helps to make the thorns ineffective.
- The okapi is the giraffe's only living family member, and it too has a prehensile blue tongue, which it uses to reach leaves and shoots high above the ground. The tongue, about 36 cm in length, is used to lick its eyelids and ears as part of its daily grooming process.
- The woodpecker has the longest tongue of any bird. It uses this elongated, thin tongue to get the tasty morsels it eats from cracks and crevices in a tree trunk. Depending on the species, its tongue can be as much as three times the length of its bill.
- The African long-tongued fruit bat lives in the tropics, in a region stretching from Guinea to Uganda. It pollinates flowers when it uses its tongue to reach the pollen and nectar on which it feeds.
- The aardvark's tongue is adapted for eating termites. It first breaks open a termite hill, and then it uses its 30-cm-tongue, covered with thick, sticky saliva, to trap the termites.
- The emperor moth begins its life with a large coiled proboscis or sucking tube which uncurls when it wants to use it to suck up nectar. When it reaches the adult stage of its life, this proboscis has dwindled away to nothing. Thus the moth is not able to feed, and eventually dies of starvation.

DID YOU KNOW?

- ◆ The elephant and the crocodile cannot stick out their tongues!
- ◆ When an elephant eats, it places the food in a hollow at the centre of its tongue, and then folds the tongue backwards into its mouth.
- ◆ The lion's tongue, which is covered in rough papillae, is used almost like sandpaper to scrape the flesh from the bones of prey. The lion also uses its tongue to 'wash' itself, much like the cats we keep as pets.

Blitzed!

The chameleon will never be used as a poster animal for the Formula One circuit, but when it comes to tongue speed, it will give all other contenders some serious competition. In fact, its tongue moves so fast that special high-speed photography was needed to determine precisely what happens in the jiffy it takes to strike. It appears that the chameleon uses suction rather than the stickiness of its tongue to catch its prey. Its tongue twists when it shoots out, forming a suction cup at the tip in the millisecond before it strikes its prey. This suction cup fastens onto the unfortunate victim and drags it back into the chameleon's mouth. Its tongue is very strong, enabling the chameleon to draw relatively large insects into its mouth where they are quickly crushed by its powerful jaws.

DID YOU KNOW?

◆ *A chameleon's tongue is twice the length of its body.*
◆ *The chameleon's name comes from the Greek 'khamaileõn', a word which means 'lion on the ground'.*

Tasty tongue tales

● A snail's tongue is called a radula. It is covered with many rows of teeth. The 20 000 teeth have flattened surfaces and the snail uses its radula to scrape off small pieces of food which it sucks into its body.
● Parrots hold and manipulate nuts, fruit and seeds with their feet. Their mouths are dry because they have no salivary glands, and they use their rubbery tongues like a thumb to take nuts out of shells.
● A pig's tongue contains 15 000 taste buds.
● The rabbit's tongue contains 17 000 taste buds.
● A snake's tongue has no taste buds. The tongue is used to bring smells and tastes into the mouth, where they are detected in two pits, the so-called 'Jacobson's organs', in the roof of the mouth. Receptors in these pits transmit smell and taste information to the brain.

An upside-down meal

The flamingo has an interesting way of feeding. Because it is a filter feeder, it puts its head upside down into the water and moves it from side to side.

It moves its very large tongue to the back of its mouth to suck in water that contains food. Then it pushes its tongue forward to force water out again. Food is trapped in the fine hairs around the beak and the flamingo can swallow it.

Ancient Romans ate flamingo tongues and considered them a delicacy!

It tastes different ...

- A butterfly has chemoreceptors, or taste receptors, on its feet.
- Blowflies taste with the 3 000 sensory hairs on their feet.
- A bee's chemoreceptors are on its jaws, forelimbs and antennae.
- An earthworm's entire body is covered with chemoreceptors.
- A housefly tastes with its feet, which are 10 million times more sensitive to taste than a human tongue.
- A catfish has approximately 100 000 taste buds, compared to a human's 10 000.

A scaly fellow

What about the pangolin or scaly anteater? It does not have any teeth at all and can't chew its food, but it loves to feast on ants and termites that are sometimes hidden away in the depths of a cleverly constructed anthill.

The pangolin uses its 25-cm tongue to get at these delicacies. Its tongue is not attached to its hyoid bone and stretches past its pharynx into the thorax.

A large salivary gland in its chest coats its tongue with the sticky saliva that it uses to trap ants.

A *good reason to be afraid*

- Cobras are able to kill immediately after they are born.
- The black-necked cobra, which lives mostly in Africa, spits its venom into the eyes of its victim and in so doing, causes blindness.
- The venom of a female black widow spider is more potent than that of a rattlesnake.
- And remember: snake venom is 90% protein.

Dangerous beasts

- Of all the animals in Africa, hippos cause the most unnatural deaths each year. Hippos run faster than humans and they are very territorial.
- The insect responsible for the most human deaths worldwide is the mosquito. The disease-carrying mosquito, carrier of encephalitis, the West Nile virus, malaria and dengue fever, is by far the deadliest creature in the animal world.
- The World Health Organization says mosquitoes cause more than two million deaths a year worldwide. Another insect, the honeybee, kills more people worldwide than all the poisonous snakes combined.

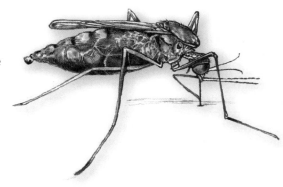

- The tsetse fly kills a further 66 000 people annually.
- The housefly is a carrier of diseases such as typhoid fever, cholera, dysentery and anthrax.

The amazing brain

The human brain has about 100 billion neurons. Compared to this ...

- There are about 300 million neurons in the octopus brain.
- Leeches have about 10 000 neurons.
- The brain of the fly contains 337 856 neurons.

More brainy facts

- A leech has 32 brains.
- Starfish haven't got any brains.
- The brain of a reptile makes up no more than 1% of the reptile's body mass.
- Octopuses have brains in their legs! They can delegate some thought processes from their central brain to smart nerves in their tentacles.
- Woodpeckers don't get headaches from all that pecking. Their skulls have air pockets to cushion the brain.
- The stegosaurus, one of the most famous dinosaurs, was an impressive 9 m long, but its brain was the size of a walnut.
- Sharks have a large, complex brain that is relative in size to that of birds.

Fun facts

The sponge is the only multicellular animal without a nervous system.
The octopus and squid belong to the class of animals known as
'Cephalopoda', meaning 'head-footed'.

The human brain

- Humans have the largest brains in relation to body size.
- An adult human male's brain makes up about 2% of his total body weight.
- The heaviest human brain ever recorded weighed about 2 300 g, but the average human brain weighs about 1 400 g. And the brain of the great physicist Albert Einstein? It weighed only 1 230 g.
- But ... after the age of 30 the brain shrinks a quarter of a per cent (0,25%) in mass each year!

DID YOU KNOW?

- A jellyfish has no brain.
- Approximately 80% of the dragonfly's brain is devoted to processing visual information.
- The oesophagus goes right through the brain of an octopus.
- The brain of a goldfish makes up 0,3% of its total body weight.

A larger brain

- The elephant has the largest brain of any land mammal.
- A bull's brain weighs between 4,2 and 5,4 kg, and the cow's brain weighs anything from 3,6 to 4,3 kg.
- The elephant's brain lies at the back of its head, far away from the front of its skull.
- The brain weighs about 1/500th of the elephant's body weight, while a human brain weighs about 1/50th of a man's body weight.

A very small brain

An ostrich is one of the world's largest land animals, yet its brain is smaller than its eye! This is because of the small brain cavity in the skull of the ostrich and the need for a large field of vision to watch for predators.

Besides humans, the 10 most intelligent animals are:

- Chimpanzee
- Gorilla
- Orang-utan
- Baboon
- Gibbon
- Monkey (especially the macaque)
- Smaller toothed whale (especially the killer whale or orca)
- Dolphin
- Elephant
- Pig

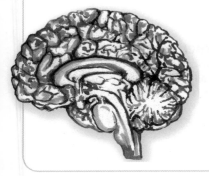

RELATIVE BRAIN WEIGHTS		
Species	Brain weight	Relative brain weight (%)
Blue whale	4 700 g	0,007
Hippopotamus	580 g	0,05
Cattle	540 g	0,07
Elephant	4 925 g	0,08
Ostrich	40 g	0,08
Gorilla	430–650 g	0,2
Lion	222 g	0,2
Horse	590 g	0,25
Wolf	114,4 g	0,52
Dog	135 g	0,59
Chimpanzee	350–400 g	0,8
Cat	31,4 g	0,94
Dolphin	700 g	1,17
Rat	3,05 g	1,22
Human	1 200–1 500 g	2–2,5
Mouse	0,4 g	3,2

Moby Dick – a brainy, toothed giant

- Moby Dick, the central character in Herman Melville's famous book, is a white or albino sperm whale.
- The sperm whale's brain is the largest and heaviest brain of any modern or extinct animal.
- A sperm whale's head is about a third of its body length. That leaves plenty of room for its brain, which could weigh as much as 7 kg, about six times more than the average human brain.
- The sperm whale is the largest mammal with teeth. Its average length is 18 m, but it can grow a lot larger. A sperm whale bull that measured 20,7 m was caught in 1950 and the lower jaw of a bull that was nearly 25,6 m long is exhibited in the British Museum.
- A sperm whale has between 20 and 26 pairs of cone-shaped teeth in its lower jaw. Each tooth is between 8 and 20 cm long and can weigh as much as 1 kg. The upper jaw does have teeth, but these never grow through the gums.

Dive, dive, dive!

In August 1969 a bull sperm whale was killed in South African waters after a dive lasting 1 hour and 52 minutes. Its stomach contents included two small sharks, a species of dogfish found only on the sea floor. The ocean floor in this region is deeper than 3 193 m in an area with a radius of 48 to 64 km. This has led scientists to believe that a sperm whale can look for food at depths of more than 3 000 m.

DID YOU KNOW?

- *The other name for the sperm whale is 'cachalot', from the Portuguese* cachalote, *which is probably a colloquial term for 'head'.*
- *In years past, spermaceti oil – obtained from the sperm whale – was used as transmission oil in Rolls-Royces.*

Another brainy fish

The African elephant-trunk fish is all brain. Its grey matter accounts for 3,1% of its body weight, which means that it needs more than 50% of its oxygen intake to sustain its brain activity.

African place names

The importance of nature in African culture is clearly illustrated by the many countries that have been named after natural features.

Islands

- **Algeria** was named after Algiers, its capital, which is known as *Al-Jazâ'ir* in Arabic and as *Alger* in French. It means 'The Islands' and refers to four islands along the coast, which were joined to the mainland from 1525.
- **The Comoros** gets its name from the Arabic *Djaza'ir al Qamar*, meaning 'Islands of the Moon'. It was originally an Arabic name given to the constellation known as the Magellanic Clouds, which indicates the direction south, and which was commonly used for all the islands in the southern latitudes, including Madagascar.

Oceans and seas

- **Benin** was named after the Bay of Benin, part of the Atlantic Ocean. Benin, a historic kingdom in Nigeria, took its name from its inhabitants, the Bini, who still occupy southern sections of Nigeria. Nigeria has a Benin City and a Benin Province. Bini is said to come from the Arabic word *banî,* meaning 'sons'.
- **Djibouti** was named after the lower part of the Gulf of Tadjoura. It was possibly derived from the Afar word *gabouri* or *gabouti,* a rug or doormat made of doum palm fibre.
- **Eritrea** was named by Italian colonists after the ancient Greek name for the Red Sea, *Erythrea Thalassa*.

Animal names

- **Cameroon** is a Portuguese word meaning 'shrimps'. In the 15th century, Portuguese explorers called the Wouri River *Rio de Camarões* ('river of shrimps'), because it teemed with these small crustaceans.
- **Côte d'Ivoire** is a French name, meaning 'Ivory Coast'. The Portuguese began to trade ivory here as early as the 16th century.

Geographical features

- The **Cape Verde** Islands were named after Cabo Verde or Cap-Vert (Green Cape) in Senegal. This cape is the westernmost point on the African continent. Portuguese explorers used the name to describe the contrast between the coast's green palm trees and sand.
- The **Central African Republic** was named after its geographical location on the continent.
- **South Africa** is the other African country that was named for its geographical location.
- **Equatorial Guinea** was named after the equator, even though the equator does not run through the country. Its southern border is 1° north of the equator.

... more African place names

Lakes

- **Chad** gets its name from this large body of water. The Arabic word *tšād* was derived from an indigenous word meaning 'large expanse of water', in other words, a 'lake'.
- **Malawi** was also named after the lake that is its dominating feature. It means 'flaming water', referring possibly to the sun's reflection on the water.
- **Tanzania** was originally known as 'Tanganyika' and 'Zanzibar', and the merging of the two resulted in the country's present name. Tanganyika is the prominent lake that borders the country. According to Sir Richard Burton, who discovered the lake in 1858, the name means 'to join', because the lake is a place where waters meet. Henry Stanley, another explorer, said it came from *tonga* (island) and *hika* (flat).

Rivers

- The **Democratic Republic of the Congo** and the **Republic of the Congo** were both named after the giant river flowing through central Africa. The name means 'mountain' and refers to the mountainous area along the river's course.
- **Gabon** gets its name from Gabao, the Portuguese name for the Mbe River. *Gabao* is a coat with a cape or hood, because the river mouth resembles this garment.
- **The Gambia** was named by Portuguese explorers who called it *Ba-Dimma*, a word used by local people for the largest river in the region. The word simply means 'river'.
- **Niger** was originally the name of a river in West Africa, which was called *nahr al-nahur* by early Arab explorers. It was a translation of the Tuareg term *egeeou n-igereouen*, which means 'river of rivers'.
- **Nigeria** was also named after the Niger River.
- **Senegal** was, like many other African countries, named after its most prominent river, the Sénégal, a name which is said to come from a local African word that means 'navigable'.
- **Togo**, which literally means 'the waterside', was probably derived from the Éwé words *to* (water) and *go* (shore).
- **Zambia** was named after the Zambezi River. The word *za* means 'river'.

Mountains

- **Kenya** was named after Mount Kenya, a name which is said to come from the Kamba, who called it *Kima ja Kegnia* (or maybe *Kinyaa* or *Kiinyaa*), meaning 'Mountain of Whiteness'. The Kikuyu name is *Kirinyaga* (or *Kere-Nyaga*), which means 'Mountain of Whiteness' or 'Mountain of Brightness'.
- **Sierra Leone** is an adapted form of the Spanish expression, *Sierra León*, which comes from the Portuguese name *Serra da Leôa* (Lion Mountains). The Portuguese navigator Pedro de Sintra recorded the name in 1462.

All desert?

According to *Guinness World Records 2007*, Africa is the continent most affected by desertification (the transformation of arable land to desert), and two-thirds of the continent has been reduced to desert or dryland.

The world's oldest desert

Namibia is home to the Namib Desert, which gets its name from a Nama word that is said to mean 'place where there is nothing'. It is the oldest desert on earth, and the only desert that provides a habitat for the elephant, lion, rhinoceros and giraffe.

The world's largest desert

Africa has the largest desert, the Sahara Desert of North Africa, which covers a total area of about 9,1 million km². It stretches 5 150 km from east to west, and from north to south its width varies from 1 280 to 2 250 km. This enormous desert expands by 0,8 km per month!

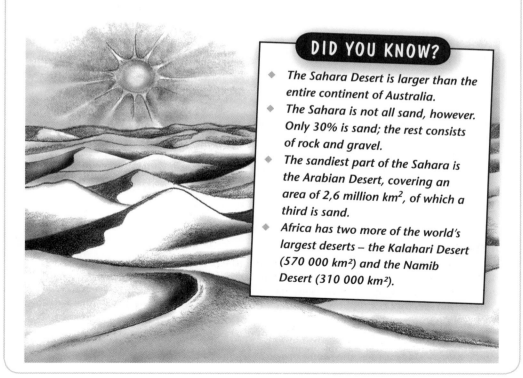

DID YOU KNOW?

- The Sahara Desert is larger than the entire continent of Australia.
- The Sahara is not all sand, however. Only 30% is sand; the rest consists of rock and gravel.
- The sandiest part of the Sahara is the Arabian Desert, covering an area of 2,6 million km², of which a third is sand.
- Africa has two more of the world's largest deserts – the Kalahari Desert (570 000 km²) and the Namib Desert (310 000 km²).

The biggest oasis

The world's largest oasis (first used by ancient Egyptians) is the Nile Valley and Nile Delta, which covers approximately 22 000 km². Oasis means 'dwelling place'.

Towering sand dunes

The world's largest, hottest desert is where you would expect the world's highest sand dunes. The dunes of Isaouane-n-Tifernine in east-central Algeria can be as high as 465 m – higher than New York's Empire State Building.

Some like it hot!

The Sahara Desert's scavenger ant scurries around in temperatures of more than 55°C, but because it moves so quickly across the sand, its exposure to the heat of the sun is reduced a lot.

When the heat gets just too much, it will rest a while on plant stalks, where the temperature is lower. Another useful feature is the ant's long legs, which can raise its body by as much as 4 mm from the searing sand, where the temperature is a few degrees cooler.

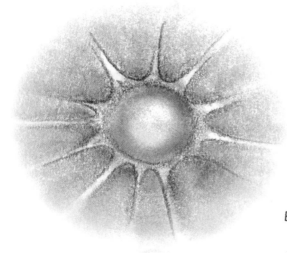

So hot!

The Sahara Desert is where the world's highest temperature has been recorded, on 13 September 1922, at Al 'Aziziyah in Libya, when the mercury soared to 57,8°C in the shade.
The highest average temperature was also recorded in Africa. The average temperature at Dallol in Ethiopia (based on readings from 1960 to 1966) was 34°C.

Destroy! Destroy!

The dry and semi-arid regions of Africa are home to extremely destructive desert locusts. These insects are quite small, only about 4,5 to 6 cm long, but each one of them can devour their own weight in food – every day.

In certain weather conditions, incredible numbers of desert locusts will gather in huge swarms and cut a swathe through all vegetation before them.

The daily food for a relatively 'small' swarm of about 50 million locusts would be enough for 500 people for a whole year!

Africa's water wonders

Africa does not consist of just sandy wastes. It has spectacular water features as well. Let's begin with the water surrounding the continent.

Africa's seas and oceans

- The Atlantic Ocean covers an area of more than 106 million km² (24% of the earth's ocean areas) and has a coastline of 111 866 km. The average depth is 3 926 m.
- The Indian Ocean has a surface area of more than 73 million km² (20% of the earth's ocean area), a coastline of 66 526 km and an average depth of about 4 210 m.
- The Red Sea is 2 330 km long and 362 km wide, with a surface area of about 450 000 km².
- The Mediterranean Sea has an area of 2 500 000 km², with an average depth of 1 500 m.

Still the longest river

The Nile is generally regarded as the world's longest river. Its total length, together with all its tributaries, is 6 695 km. The Amazon is believed to be 6 448 km long.

The lengths of the Amazon and the Nile have been the subject of many disputes over the past century, especially since rivers' lengths are affected by seasonal changes. Even reputable sources disagree as to the actual length of these two great rivers.

In the 20th century the Nile has generally been regarded as the world's longest river, with a length of anywhere between 5 499 and 6 690 km, while the Amazon's length varies between 6 259 and 6 712 km.

In June 2007 a team of scientists claimed to have found the Amazon's source in Peru, which will make it 6 800 km long. As this still has to be verified before it is generally accepted, the debate will rage on …

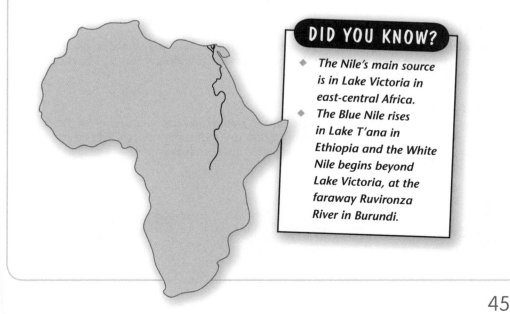

DID YOU KNOW?

- The Nile's main source is in Lake Victoria in east-central Africa.
- The Blue Nile rises in Lake T'ana in Ethiopia and the White Nile begins beyond Lake Victoria, at the faraway Ruvironza River in Burundi.

... more African water wonders

A man-made sea

Lake Volta in Ghana is the artificial or man-made lake with the largest surface area. It was formed when the Akosombo Dam was completed in 1965. Within four years, the lake had covered an area of 8 482 km², which is just smaller than the island of Cyprus, and about 145 times as big as New York's Manhattan Island!

An underground sea

The cave known as Drachenrauchloch (Dragon's Breath Hole), near Grootfontein in Namibia, was discovered in 1986 and contains the world's largest known underground lake, about 66 m underground. The lake covers an area of 2,61 ha.

The waterfall with the largest flow

The waterfall with the largest average annual flow is the Boyoma Falls in the Democratic Republic of the Congo, with a flow of 17 000 m³/sec.

Nearly a kilometre high

KwaZulu-Natal's Thukela Falls, the world's second highest waterfall, consists of five major falls, of which the highest is a sheer drop of 411 m. The total drop is 948 m.

The largest pink lake

Lac Rose (Pink Lake, also known as Retba Lake) is a shallow lagoon north of Dakar in Senegal. When the water level is low, it has a surface area of 5 by 1,5 km. And why is it pink? Oh, that's caused by micro-organisms and strong concentrations of minerals.

Most thunder

If you suffer from ceraunophobia, astraphobia or astrapophobia, you should steer clear of Tororo in Uganda. It is the place with the most days with thunderstorms – 251 days per year for the decade 1967 to 1976.

The largest swamp

The Okavango Swamp, the world's largest inland swamp, has a surface area of 16 835 km², although it may expand to a maximum of 22 000 km² in the rainy season. The swamp has formed over the past two million years, mainly because of silt sediments that seeped into the flat, dry landscape of northern Botswana.

... other water wonders

A freshwater giant

Lake Victoria, which lies between Tanzania and Uganda, approximately 1 130 m above sea level, is the world's second largest freshwater lake by surface area. (The largest is Lake Superior in the USA.)

Lake Victoria, which is 322 km long and about 240 km wide, has a surface area of 69 485 km². It is slightly smaller than Ireland or Sierra Leone.

Another large river
The Congo River, 4 670 km long, is:

- the largest river in Western Central Africa
- the second longest river in Africa
- the eighth longest river in the world.

> **DID YOU KNOW?**
>
> When the Congo empties into the Atlantic Ocean it flows 800 km further into the ocean, in a submarine canyon that is more than 1 200 m deep.

The world's longest lake

Lake Tanganyika is the world's longest lake (680 km long), with an average width of 50 km. Its width varies from 16 km to 72 km.

The maximum depth is 1 436 m, and it holds seven times more fresh water than Lake Victoria.

Lake Tanganyika is not only one of the oldest known lakes, but it holds a number of other records. It is the ...

- largest rift lake in Africa
- longest freshwater lake in the world
- largest lake, by volume of fresh water, in Africa
- deepest lake in Africa
- second deepest lake in the world, after Lake Baikal in Russia
- second deepest freshwater lake in the world, after Lake Baikal
- second largest lake in the world by volume, after Lake Baikal
- second largest lake in Africa, by surface area
- seventh largest lake in the world, by surface area.

Hot and cold at the same time

Lake Bogoria in Kenya is a lake of extremes – scalding hot in some places and icy cold in others. The water in the springs on its shores is so hot that you can cook eggs in it.

A Californian company bought enzyme samples from Lake Bogoria, patented them and cloned them for use by textile companies and detergent manufacturers. An enzyme from this lake is used in bleach for clothes such as stonewashed jeans, while another enzyme is used in detergents.

... yet more water wonders

The incredible shrinking lake

Lake Chad lies between four countries – Chad, Cameroon, Niger and Nigeria. It was once (between 15 000 and 25 000 years ago) an enormous inland sea, covering 400 000 km² and draining into the Atlantic Ocean.

In recent years its surface area has varied dramatically. About 40 years ago it was Africa's fourth largest lake, with an area of more than 26 000 km², but since 2000 it has sometimes shrunk to less than 1 500 km².

DID YOU KNOW?

Kenya's Lake Nakuru, a small, shallow, alkaline, saline lake in Africa's Eastern Rift Valley, is home to nearly 500 bird species. One of these, the lesser flamingo, feeds on the blue-green algae in the lake, which gives them their pink colour.

Lake in a depression

Lake Assal, a crater lake in the Danakil Desert, lies 155 m below sea level in Djibouti's Afar Depression, the lowest point in Africa, and the third-lowest geographical point in the world. Because no rivers flow out of it, it has a salinity level of 35%, the most saline body of water in the world – ten times saltier than the ocean.

The caustic red lake

- The bright red Lake Natron in northern Tanzania is the world's most caustic body of water.
- The lake's warm water and shores provide the only breeding place in Eastern Africa for 2,5 million lesser flamingos, because it is too caustic for predators.
- The water contains spirulina, the blue-green algae with red pigment.
- The mud is very hot, and can reach temperatures as high as 60°C, while the alkalinity can have a pH as high as 10,5.

The deadliest lake

Lake Nyos is a 200-m-deep lake in western Cameroon. In August 1986 a mixture of carbon dioxide (CO_2) and water erupted from the lake's surface at a speed of about 100 km/h, forming a 50-m-thick poisonous cloud of carbon dioxide that rolled into the valleys on the north side of the crater at a speed of up to 50 km/h. It caused the deaths of more than 1 700 people, as well as many animals and birds.

A large island

Madagascar, with an area of 587 041 km², is the world's fourth largest island. The three largest islands are Greenland, Borneo and Nieu Guinea.

A convergence of points

Cape Three Points, in the Gulf of Guinea, is the closest place on earth to the point where 0° longitude (Greenwich meridian) and 0° latitude (the equator) meet at 0 m (sea level).

Madagascar is about the same size as countries like Kenya or Botswana.

DID YOU KNOW?

The Fish River Canyon is the world's second largest canyon, after the Grand Canyon in the USA.

The largest rift

The great African Rift Valley, the world's largest rift valley, extends over a total distance of 6 400 km, from Syria in southwest Asia to Mozambique in southeast Africa. Its width ranges between a few kilometres to more than 160 km. It splits into two branches in East Africa: the Eastern Rift Valley and the Western Rift Valley.

Elephant proverbs

'An elephant's tusks are never too heavy for it.' Zimbabwe
'You must eat an elephant one bite at a time.' Twi
'People helping one another can bring an elephant into the house.' Rwanda
'When elephants fight, it is the grass that suffers.' Kikuyu
'The tracks of the elephant cancel those of the antelope.' Duala

Born with horns

- A giraffe is the only animal born with horns. At birth these small horns, which are not yet attached to the skull, are neatly folded back on the head. They will only move into an upright position a while later.
- The bull's horns are thick, and early in his life they are about 13,5 cm long. They keep growing until they are about 30 cm long. At that time they have bare tops with hair tassels around the tips.
- The cow's horns are thinner. As the giraffe matures, calcium deposits form on the skull and more horn-like bumps appear.
- Sometimes there are three bumps, two on the back of the head and one on the forehead.
- The skull grows heavier as the giraffe matures. After 10 years, the skull is 7 kg heavier than when the animal was born.

More giraffe facts

- The giraffe's lungs can each hold 55 litres of air.
- The calf's neck is only a sixth of its body length at birth, but within four years it grows to a third of its total length.

Monkeys? Apes? Baboons? Lemurs?

What is the difference between an ape and a monkey and a baboon?

- **An ape** is a large primate with a complex brain and no tail, such as the gorilla, bonobo and chimpanzee. The chimpanzee and gorilla, the so-called great apes, can walk upright but prefer to travel on all fours, with their knuckles touching the ground. Apes also have appendixes!
- **A monkey** has a tail, usually lives in trees and moves on all fours, although it can stand on two legs for short periods of time.
- Old World monkeys include the beautifully coloured African guenon, mangabey and colobus, macaques, such as the Barbary ape of North Africa, as well as the coloured African drills and mandrills.
- **The baboon** is a member of the monkey family, just like the vervet monkey.
- **The lemur** is a member of another primate family, found only on Madagascar and the Comoro Islands.

Bonobos – our close relatives

- Bonobos are closely related to humans, sharing 98,4% of our genetic makeup. They can be distinguished from common chimpanzees by their black faces and red lips, two or three webbed toes and, in adulthood, a prominent tail tuft.
- The long hair on their heads is parted in the middle and sweeps from the sides of their faces to cover their ears.
- Bonobos are arboreal, and spend most of their time in the canopies of tall, dense tropical forests.
- The bonobo's only habitat is in the Democratic Republic of the Congo, in a region between the Congo, Lomami, Kasai and Sankuru rivers, and Lake Tumba and Lac Ndombe.

The most colourful monkey

The male mandrill of equatorial West Africa has an average head and body length of 61 to 76 cm. Its tail is quite short, only 5 to 7 cm. The adult male weighs an average of 25 kg, although a large mandrill can weigh as much as 54 kg. The mandrill is one of the most colourful mammals known, with a naked blue rump, red-striped face and yellow beard.

DID YOU KNOW?

◆ The naked mole-rat has very little hair, and its skin is wrinkly and pink or greyish-pink.

◆ It is a little digger (only 7 cm long and weighing 30 to 70 grams), with a short, broad head, powerful jaw muscles and huge incisors to cut its way through the ground. Despite its name, it is a mole, after all.

Our southernmost relatives

The southernmost non-human primates are the chacma baboons living on the Cape Peninsula in South Africa, at a latitude of 34°S.

Home, sweet home

Chimpanzees build nests in tree tops. They bend branches together and weave small twigs into the framework.

The naked little digger

The only mammal that lives in colonies (like termites and ants) is the naked mole-rat. Colonies has a caste system and a population of 20 to 300.

The only breeding female, the queen, gives birth to all the babies. She is guarded by a number of males or soldier mole-rats. The other mole-rats in the colony are workers and they dig the tunnels.

Proverbs from Africa

'Those who get to the river early drink the cleanest water.' Kenya
'A chattering bird builds no nest.' Cameroon
'All monkeys cannot hang on the same branch.' Kenya
'A camel does not joke about the hump of another camel.' Guinea
'Wind makes more noise among the trees.' Kikuyu
'The leopard's skin is beautiful, but his heart evil.' Baluba
'Hunger pushes the hippopotamus out of the water.' Luo

The sports we play

Soccer or football is an important recreational activity in Africa, and many African players are stars for clubs all over the world. A large number of African countries' national teams have chosen animal names for their teams.

Lions

The lion is an important animal in Africa, and no less than three teams have this royal animal as their team symbol. **Cameroon's** national team is known as the Indomitable Lions, while the women's team is the Indomitable Lionesses. The junior teams are called Lions Espoir (Lion Hopefuls), Junior Lions (Lions Junior) and Lionceaux (Lion Cubs).

Morocco has added one of their country's most prominent geographical features to their team's name, calling it the Lions de l'Atlas (Atlas Lions). The other team are the Atlas Lionesses, Les Lions Espoir (Lion Hopefuls), The Junior Lions and The Atlas Cubs. **Senegal** has a team known as the Lions of Teranga, while Gabon has opted for another member of the cat family, calling their team Les Panthères. The **Democratic Republic of the Congo** has simplified everything by choosing Simba (lion) as the name for their national team.

Elephants

The **Côte d'Ivoire** has decided on a fairly obvious name: Les Elephants. The Ivoire Olympique is the Olympic team, and the juniors are Les Elephanteaux Juniors and Les Elephanteaux Cadets.

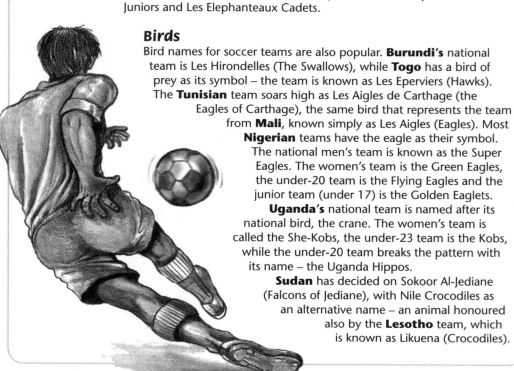

Birds

Bird names for soccer teams are also popular. **Burundi's** national team is Les Hirondelles (The Swallows), while **Togo** has a bird of prey as its symbol – the team is known as Les Eperviers (Hawks). The **Tunisian** team soars high as Les Aigles de Carthage (the Eagles of Carthage), the same bird that represents the team from **Mali**, known simply as Les Aigles (Eagles). Most **Nigerian** teams have the eagle as their symbol. The national men's team is known as the Super Eagles. The women's team is the Green Eagles, the under-20 team is the Flying Eagles and the junior team (under 17) is the Golden Eaglets.

Uganda's national team is named after its national bird, the crane. The women's team is called the She-Kobs, the under-23 team is the Kobs, while the under-20 team breaks the pattern with its name – the Uganda Hippos.

Sudan has decided on Sokoor Al-Jediane (Falcons of Jediane), with Nile Crocodiles as an alternative name – an animal honoured also by the **Lesotho** team, which is known as Likuena (Crocodiles).

All the other animals

Other animal names feature in the names of soccer teams. The **Algerian** team is Les Fennecs (The Desert Foxes), while **Benin** is Ecureuils (Squirrels), the **Botswana** team is the Zebras and **Burkina Faso** Les Etalons (Stallions). The **Central African Republic** is represented by the Low-Ubangui Fawns.

The national teams of **The Gambia** and **Madagascar** are both called Scorpions, and **Mozambique** is even more venomous – their team is known as the Mambas. **Rwanda** has another name with a sting to it: Amavubi (Wasps).

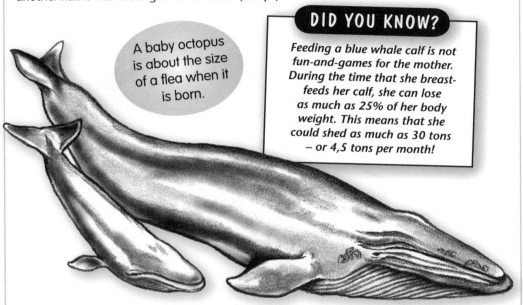

A baby octopus is about the size of a flea when it is born.

DID YOU KNOW?

Feeding a blue whale calf is not fun-and-games for the mother. During the time that she breast-feeds her calf, she can lose as much as 25% of her body weight. This means that she could shed as much as 30 tons – or 4,5 tons per month!

A tremendous growth spurt

The blue whale calf has an astonishing growth spurt. It grows for about 11 months in the mother's womb, developing from a small fertilized egg to a foetus that is 4,5 m long and weighs 15 tons. After birth, the blue whale calf's weight increases by 4,5 kg every day. That is why it has to feed 50 times per day, drinking as much as 11 litres of milk at a time. For almost a year, the blue whale mum has to produce 427 litres of milk every day to keep her voracious little feeder satisfied. In the first year of its life the little giant will grow to a length of nearly 19 m. At this age it could weigh as much as 65 tons – an increase of just less than 4 tons per month.

Growing up – slightly more leisurely

A young giraffe grows a little taller each day – a whole 0,5 cm taller, in fact. When it is born the calf is 1,8 m tall, but this height will double in its first year.

An elephant calf weighs about 120 kg at birth, and it will grow to a sturdy 1 000 kg at the age of six. That is about the same weight as an adult rhinoceros.

The miracle plant

In the 19th century Friedrich Welwitsch, an Austrian botanist, discovered an unusual plant, now named *Welwitschia mirabilis,* in southern Angola. It can reach an age of up to 2 000 years, and grows in areas where the annual rainfall is less than 25 mm.

The plant absorbs vapour from the ocean mists drifting across the desert. To prevent evaporation, the leaves' stomata open when mists drift across the desert, but close when temperatures rise.

The *Welwitschia mirabilis* has two gigantic leaves – 1,79 m wide, 6 m long and 4 mm thick. About 3,15 m of the leaf is alive. Its root can go 30 m deep into the earth.

Look, Ma, no teeth!

The blue whale is a baleen whale. It has no teeth, but a series of 260 to 400 overlapping black plates that hang from each side of its upper jaw. These plates consist of keratin, and have fine hairs inside the mouth, near the tongue. The plates in the front of the mouth are about 51 cm long, while those at the back are 102 cm long. When the whale is feeding, it takes large volumes of water and food into its mouth, and when the mouth closes, the water is expelled through the baleen plates. The food is trapped on the inside near the tongue and can be swallowed easily.

The smallest prey

The greatest difference in size between predator and prey exists between the massive blue whale, the world's largest animal, and the krill it eats. The blue whale has an average length of 25 m, while each of the tiny shrimp-like krill is about 50 mm long.

In the feeding season this gigantic animal gorges itself on about 3,6 tons of krill each day. This means that it eats about 40 million krill – per day!

A blue whale's oesophagus has a normal diameter of about 10 to 13 cm. It can expand to only 25 cm, which means that it can't swallow any large fish.

But what IS krill exactly?

- Krill is the term used for the tons of shrimp-like creatures that form the staple food of whales and other marine animals.
- Krill is a Norwegian whaling term that means 'tiny fish' – but actually they are crustaceans.
- It is a large species of plankton with a collective mass many times that of the world's whole human population.
- Humans are beginning to realize the value of this concentrated source of energy-rich food, and are beginning to use it as a food source.

The need for teeth

Mammals need their teeth to do several different jobs and so mammals' teeth have evolved into different forms. Mammal's teeth can grind, stab, scissor, dig, chisel, sieve and lift (like an elephant's tusks).

Carnivores (meat-eaters) have sharp teeth; herbivores (plant-eaters) have flat teeth. Omnivores (animals that eat both plants and meat) have sharp teeth in front and flat teeth at the back.

No need for teeth

Several groups of mammals have decided they don't need teeth. The 10 species of whales in the order *Mysticeti*, the eight species of pangolins and the three species of anteaters in the family *Myrmecophagidae* (order *Edentata*) have no teeth at all.

A mouth full of teeth

- The mammals with the most teeth come from two of the three orders that also have some of the mammals with the fewest teeth.
- The land mammal with the most teeth is the giant armadillo (order *Edentata*), which can have as many as 100 teeth in its jaws.
- In the oceans the toothiest mammal comes from the order *Odontoceti*. The dolphin can have as many as 252 teeth in its long, thin jaws. These teeth look more like reptile teeth, because all have the same basic shape – they look like thin, sharp little spears.

HOW MANY TEETH?

Species	Teeth
Pangolin	0
Whale (*Mysticeti*)	0
Anteater (*Edentata*)	0
Rat	16
Mouse	16
Porcupine	20
Squirrel	22
Elephant	26
Rhinoceros	26
Hare	28
Rabbit	28
Lynx	30
Cat	30
Lion	30
Ape	32
Horseshoe bat	32
Cattle	32
Giraffe	32
Human	32
Hyaena	32
Ibex	32
Camel	34
Hedgehog	36
Mouse-eared bat	38
Hippopotamus	40
Horse	40
Fox	42
Mole	44
Giant armadillo (*Edentata*)	100
Dolphin	252

Fun facts about teeth

- A rodent's teeth never stop growing.
- Mosquitoes have 47 teeth.
- Most snakes have more than 200 teeth.
- Toads have no teeth.
- Frogs have teeth in their upper jaws but none in their lower jaws.

DID YOU KNOW?

An adult hippo can bite a 4-m-long male crocodile in half.

Crocodile's teeth

A crocodile can open and close its jaws, but cannot move them from side to side.

At any given time a crocodile may have 60 teeth in its mouth, but it can't chew its food. That is why it follows the rip-and-shred approach and it is inevitable that some teeth will be lost along the way. The lost teeth are soon replaced, however, and a crocodile can grow up to 50 new sets of teeth (between 2 000 and 3 000) in its lifetime.

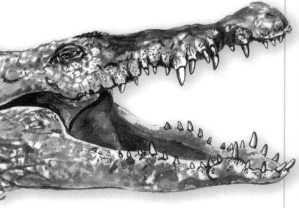

Snakes alive!

◆ Venomous snakes have hollow fangs which eject poison.

◆ The gaboon viper has the longest poison teeth and produces the most poison of all snakes. The snake reaches a length of up to 1,83 m, and its teeth can be as long as 50 mm.

◆ The saw-scaled adder (or mat adder) is responsible for the most fatal bites involving humans – more than any other snake.

Shark!

A shark can have as many as eight rows of razor-sharp teeth. As sharks are anything but gentle when they tear their prey apart, some teeth may break off in a feeding frenzy. These missing teeth are (un)fortunately constantly replaced, and some sharks can have as many as 20 000 to 30 000 teeth in a lifetime.

The largest predatory fish is the great white shark or white pointer. A fully grown great white can be between 4,3 and 4,6 m long, and weigh anything between 520 and 770 kg. This fearsome creature has up to 3 000 teeth, and can reach an age of 100 years.

Saw away!

● The sawfish is named after its saw-like external teeth that surround its sensitive snout. The sawfish swings its 'saw' from side to side to slash at its prey – often mullet and herring. It will usually swim slowly in its undulating way in shallow, muddy water, using the saw to rake the mud in search of crustaceans and other prey. This constant use wears down the teeth, but it is no problem as they keep on growing from their bases.

● Isn't it quite painful to give birth to a live saw-bearing baby? Fortunately, nature has foreseen this problem, and has covered the youngster's saw with a sheath.

● A sawfish is family of the shark, and its whole skeleton consists of cartilage. Its teeth are adapted scales.

● The sawfish detects electrical fields generated by its prey with special cells on its saw and head.

Bite me!

The instrument that was developed for measuring the force that sharks use when biting has a novel name. It is called a 'Snodgrass gnathodynamometer' (or shark-bite meter).

According to the SG (for short), a dusky shark 2 m in length exerts a force of 60 kg between its jaws. The pressure at the tips of its teeth would be 3 tons/cm².

BITE PRESSURE

With how much pressure does a fierce animal bite down? Here are a few interesting comparisons with the human bite.

Species	Bite pressure
Human	55 kg
Pit bull	108 kg
German shepherd dog	109 kg
Wild dog	144 kg
Rottweiler	149 kg
Great white shark	272 kg
Lion	318 kg
Hyaena	454 kg
Snapping turtle	456 kg
Nile crocodile	1 134 kg

Teeth first

Warthogs like to sleep and breed in abandoned aardvark dens.

When a warthog family enters its den for the night, the young go in head first and the last adult to enter the burrow does so backwards, so that its tusks are facing potential enemies.

Their tusks can rip open a lion's belly – that is why the adult will present its 'sharp end' to its enemies for as long as possible.

When it exits the burrow the next morning, it does so at full speed to get the jump on its enemies.

More warthog facts

- Warthogs live in small family groups of males and females. This family group is known as a 'sounder'.
- Warthogs have no sweat glands, so they keep cool by covering themselves in mud from waterholes.
- A warthog can reach speeds of 50 km/h.
- The warthog has a short neck and relatively long legs. That is why it has to stand on its knees when it feeds. To make this way of grazing slightly easier, it has developed horny pads on its knees.
- The warthog's eyes are set high and well back on its forehead, so that it can still look out for predators, even when it is on its knees.

Still – there's no need for teeth

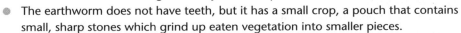

- Some snails are carnivorous, like the species of sea snail that eats clams. It can produce sulphuric acid to burn a hole in a clam's shell, through which it sucks the soft parts of the clam.
- Another sea-water snail waits until an oyster opens its shell, and it then pushes its own shell into the opening, to prevent the oyster from closing its shell. Then the snail is free to start feeding on the oyster's soft parts.
- The earthworm does not have teeth, but it has a small crop, a pouch that contains small, sharp stones which grind up eaten vegetation into smaller pieces.
- Mussels are filter feeders that eat small microscopic animals and plants in plankton. The mussel uses its muscles to create water currents through its body. It has specialized, hair-like structures to sift out plankton.
- The female mosquito has very long and thin mouthparts that can be pushed through a victim's skin.
- A butterfly and the male mosquito drink flower nectar through a proboscis, a very long mouthpart. The proboscis is coiled under the head in flight and is extended only for feeding.

A real meatfest

A male lion has a huge appetite and when the females have put some meat on the menu, it will eat 18 kg of it in one session. If it is really hungry, it will devour as much as 34 kg. After such a feast it will fall asleep – and sleep for up to 24 hours! When it wakes up it may laze around for a few days and only feel the need to go hunting after a week.

A single lion eats some 10 to 20 large animals in a year, but it is hard work for a lion to stay full, because most lion hunts fail. One study showed that only 10 in 62 hunts are successful.

DID YOU KNOW?

- ◆ *The leopard is Africa's most successful hunter with a success rate of around 40%.*
- ◆ *Kilogram for kilogram, the leopard is about seven times stronger than a human. It can drag a carcass that is more or less 3½ times heavier than itself 6 m high into a tree.*

A leopard's tail

The tip of the leopard's long tail is white underneath. When the leopard has finished hunting and has eaten its fill, it will walk between the antelope in a herd with its tail folded back so that the white shows. This white 'flag' is an indication that it is not hunting and that every animal is safe (for a while, at least!).

Seeing is believing

- The largest eye belongs to the Atlantic giant squid, which is the largest of all the world's invertebrates. One specimen found in Canada in 1878 had eyes with a diameter of 40 cm – larger than a dinner plate. One tentacle was 10,7 m long and its body measured 6,1 m.
- The giant squid's eye has a retina with as many as 1 billion photoreceptors.
- The octopus has a retina that contains 20 million photoreceptors.

A bird's eye view

- Predatory birds have the most impressive eyesight. Buzzards can spot small rodents from a height of 4 500 m. While humans have 20/20 vision, hawks have 20/5 vision. This means that the details we can see from about 1,5 m away, the hawk can see from a distance of about 6 m.
- The peregrine falcon can spot its prey from more than 8 km away.
- The golden eagle can spot a rabbit at a distance of 1,6 km.
- A buzzard's retina has 1 million photoreceptors per mm², enabling it to see small rodents from a height of 4 500 m. The sparrow's retina contains 400 000 photoreceptors per mm².
- Eagles have more than 1 million photoreceptors per mm² in their retinas; humans have 200 000 photoreceptors per mm².
- The vision of some species of eagle is 2,0 to 3,6 times better than that of humans.
- A falcon's vision is 2,6 times better than that of a human. It can see a 10 cm object from a distance of 1,5 km and it can even see sharp images when it is diving at 160 km/h.
- The eagle's eyeball is 35 mm long, compared to the human eyeball's length of 24 mm.

- *The eyes of a bird of prey stare straight ahead, because its eyeballs are too large to swivel. It has to turn its head to look to either side.*
- *Birds use their left and right eyes for different purposes. They use the left eye to pick up colours and the right to detect movement.*
- *An owl's eyes are bigger than its brain. The owl is the only bird that can see the colour blue.*

Keep your eye on it

- The pigeon has its eyes mounted laterally on its head so that it can see for an impressive 340° around it – everywhere, in fact, except the back of its own head.
- A chameleon can move its eyes in two different directions at the same time, so that it can spot predators more easily.
- A sea horse's eyes are mounted on small turrets. Each turret can turn in a different direction, so that a sea horse can keep one eye open for food and the other for danger.
- Many crabs have their eyes on the ends of stalks.

The eyes have it!

- Scallops have 100 eyes around the edges of their shells, probably to detect shadows of predators.
- A starfish's arms are covered with light-sensitive cells, and light projected on an 'eyespot' on each arm causes the arm to move.
- Spiders usually have eight eyes, but some can have up to a dozen eyes and others have no eyes at all. Most spiders can only tell the difference between light and dark.
- Box jellyfish have 24 eyes and four brains.
- A scorpion can have as many as 12 eyes.
- The dragonfly's eye contains 30 000 lenses.
- Bees and butterflies can see ultraviolet light.

Night vision

- Geckos and moths see colours in the dark.
- Catfish use night vision to track their prey in pitch-black waters – they just follow the chemical traces that other fish leave behind.
- Some fish can see into the infrared wavelength of the electromagnetic spectrum.
- A deep-sea fish's retina has only rods – 25 million rods/mm^2. This high density of photoreceptors could be necessary to detect the dim bio-luminescence that exists in the ocean depths.
- Sharks can detect the dimmest light sources under the water – even a glow 10 times dimmer than anything the human eye can see.

Sea turtles absorb a lot of salt from sea water and when they excrete the excess salt from their eyes, it often looks as if they're crying.

Strange shapes

- The octopus eye has a rectangular pupil, but no cornea.
- The pupil in the eye of the giant cuttlefish (a squid-like animal) is also rectangular.
- A goat's eyes have rectangular pupils.
- The owl's eyeballs are tubular in shape – that is why the bird cannot move its eyes.
- The penguin has a flat cornea that allows for clear vision underwater. Penguins can also see into the ultraviolet range of the electromagnetic spectrum.

The all-seeing eye

A stomatopod (such as the mantis shrimp) has a spectacular range of colour vision.

Scientists compare colour vision in different animals by counting the colour photoreceptors in their eyes. Most mammals have two types, but primates (the order which includes humans) have three. Most birds and reptiles have four. Stomatopods have at least eight and can detect many colours and thousands of shades of these colours in the ultraviolet waveband (which people can't see at all). It is especially useful in coral reefs, where colour is commonly used as camouflage.

Stomatopods have polarization vision that is more complex than anything that can be created with photography. Their compound eyes, with thousands of elements, are on stalks and can move independently through 360°.

This helps the stomatopod to see objects in depth by observing them from three angles. This means that stomatopods, like the mantis shrimp, have trinocular vision in a single eye.

Going batty

Using its 'nose-leaf', a bat can detect an animal's body heat from about 16 m away. Bats use their sense of echolocation to find an insect and get information about the type of insect – from a distance of up to 5,5 m away.

Animal senses – insect detection

- Ants can detect small movements through 5 cm of earth.
- What attracts a mosquito to a human body? Body odour (especially from the feet!), carbon dioxide, body heat and body humidity.
- Worker honey bees have a ring of iron oxide or magnetite in their abdomens to detect magnetic fields. This can help them to detect changes in the earth's magnetic field, which is quite useful for navigation.
- The hairs on a butterfly's wings help it to detect changes in air pressure.
- A cockroach can detect movement as small as 2 000 times the diameter of a hydrogen atom.
- The grasshopper has hairs (called 'sensilla') all over its body to detect air movements.
- The emperor moth can detect pheromones as far away as 5 km, while the silkworm moth can detect pheromones over a distance of up to 11 km. It can detect these pheromones in concentrations as low as one molecule of pheromone per 10^{17} molecules of air.

Under the sea

- Fish can detect L-serine, a chemical found in the skin of mammals, even if it is diluted to one part per billion.
- Fish have a 'lateral line' system, consisting of sense organs or 'neuromasts', located in canals along the head and trunk. They use these receptors to detect changes in water pressure, to locate prey and help with their movement.
- The drum fish detects underwater sound vibrations with an air bladder. Signals are sent from the air bladder to its middle ear and then to the inner ear, where hair cells respond to the vibration and transmit sound information to the brain.
- The shark has specialized electro-sensing receptors with thresholds as low as 0,005 uV/cm. These receptors may be used to locate prey.
- Catfish have three or four pairs of whiskers, called barbels, to help them find food.

Detectives of a different kind

- A scorpion has special hairs on its pincers, which can detect air moving at as little as 0,072 km/h.
- The crab detects water currents and vibrations with the hairs on its claws and other parts of its body.
- Crayfish have sensory hairs that help it to detect movement of 0,1 micron at a frequency of 100 Hz.
- An octopus has chemoreceptors on the suckers of its tentacles. By tasting this way, an octopus does not have to leave the safety of its home.
- Dolphins use echolocation for detecting movement and locating objects.
- The dogfish can detect a flounder that is buried under the sand and emitting four milliampere of current.

Snake sense

Pit-vipers have a heat-sensitive organ, about 0,5 cm deep, between their eyes and nostrils. This organ has a membrane with 7 000 nerve endings that respond to temperature changes as small as 0,002 to 0,003°C.

The five senses

How would a human's five senses compare to the rest of the animal world?

- Vision? A human can see a candle flame 48 km away – if it is a dark, clear night.
- Hearing? A human can hear a watch ticking 6 m away – if it is in a quiet place.
- Taste? A human can taste a teaspoon of sugar in 7,5 litres of water.
- Smell? A human can smell a single drop of perfume in a three-room apartment.
- Touch? A human can feel on its cheek the wing of a bee falling from a distance of 1 cm.

DID YOU KNOW?

Compared to humans, houseflies are 10 million times more sensitive to the taste of sugar.

Shark senses

- Sharks have a fantastic sense of smell. Fish extracts with concentrations of only one part per 10 billion parts of water can alter a shark's behaviour.
- Sharks can detect water movement through a series of pit organs (the lateral line system) located under their skin.
- Sharks can detect pressure that depresses their skin only 10 millionths of a metre.

Hearty appetites

- The female horsefly is not particular – it will attack any animal, using its knife-like jaws to extract the blood it needs. Its saliva will stop the blood clotting. Male horseflies are not a danger to humans and animals, because they drink only plant nectar.
- Spiders don't chew their food. The saliva they inject into their prey dissolves its insides and the spider then just sucks up its liquid meal.

Nearly a quarter of all mammals can fly! There are 985 species of bats, which make up 23,1% of all species of known mammals.

Remarkable regeneration

Sponges have the most remarkable powers of regeneration of any animal. If they lose a segment of their bodies, it grows right back. In fact, if a sponge should be forced through a fine-meshed silk gauze, the separate fragments can re-form again into a sponge.

The world's deadliest animal – after humans

The world's most dangerous animals (excluding humans!) are malaria parasites (of the genus *Plasmodium*) which are carried by Anopheles mosquitoes.

It is estimated that these minute assassins have been directly or indirectly responsible for 50% of all human deaths since the Stone Age.

Today, at least 200 million people contract the disease every year, and every year it causes the deaths of more than one million babies and children in Africa alone.

What a croc!

- When crocodiles yawn, they are not tired or bored. The open jaws help them to cool down.
- The female crocodiles lay their eggs in sand, away from water. When little crocodiles hatch, the mother scoops them up in her large jaws and carries them to the water.
- A crocodile has three eyelids – one at the top of the eye, one at the bottom, and a clear eyelid to protect the eye when the crocodile is under the water.
- The crocodile has tear glands which produce a liquid when the animal has been out of the water for a while. That's where the expression 'crocodile tears' comes from.

Puffing it up

The pufferfish can perform some extraordinary tricks when it feels threatened.

The first is to blow itself up to three times its normal size by sucking sea water as fast as it can into its stomach, which is normally folded up in neat pleats.

When its body is inflated like this, the scales unfold into hundreds of sharp spines or quills that will be enough to make any potential attacker lose its appetite.

The big question is what happens to the food in its stomach? No problem. The food passes straight through the stomach to the intestines.

The heaviest flier

The kori bustard is not a very willing flier, but when it is threatened it will take to the air and become the heaviest flying bird. It will also migrate locally by an aerial route, but for every other purpose it will walk or run.

And how heavy is the kori bustard? A male can weigh as much as 19 kg, which is heavier than its closest rivals for the title, which include the Andean condor, wandering albatross and swan, all of which will tip the scales at a maximum of 15 kg.

By the way, the kori bustard is a lot lighter than its prehistoric predecessors, like the giant teratorn, which could easily weigh 80 kg.

The slithering blitz

◆ The black mamba is the largest venomous snake in Africa.

◆ It gets its name not from its colour (which varies from pale grey to black), but from the black inside its mouth. According to those who have seen it, this open mouth is not something anybody would like to see more than once!

◆ The black mamba is the world's fastest snake. It can slither along at a speed of 17 km/h, which is not even half the speed of the human world record holder in the 100 m. So it will be quite possible for even a slow human to outrun a black mamba.

Swiftly, swiftly through the air

The swift is an exceptional flier, but it can't walk because its legs and feet are just not built for it. If it should be on the ground, it wouldn't be able to launch itself into the air again.

It doesn't need to walk, though, because it spends most of its life on the wing, flying great distances and eating, drinking, mating and even sleeping while it is airborne.

In its first year it doesn't attempt to fly north to nest, which means it stays in the air for its first two years. In this time it flies a distance that is the same as from the earth to the moon and back.

Passing a jet plane

The peregrine falcon is the world's fastest flying bird. When it swoops down on its prey, it regularly reaches speeds of up to 290 km/h, and there is filmed evidence of a bird plummeting down at 322 km/h.

To achieve this, it free-falls, sometimes for more than a kilometre, so that it can (theoretically) reach speeds of 385 km/h.

The peregrine falcon's swoop is called 'stooping' or 'plunge-diving'.

The next generation

At what age is a mammal mature enough to start thinking about the next generation? It differs a lot from one species to the next. A rat will be ready for a spot of procreation at an age of between two and three months, while the rhinoceros can take as long as 20 years to prepare for this important transition.

AGE OF SEXUAL MATURITY

Species	Age	Species	Age
Rat	2–3 months	Common frog	3 years
Mouse	2–6 months	Horse	3–4 years
Rabbit	5–9 months	Ostrich	3–4 years
Hare	6 months	Salamander	3–4 years
Domestic pig	7 months	Anura	3–4 years
Bushbaby	8 months	Lion	3–5 years
Fox	10 months	Bird of prey	3–6 years
Cat	1 year	Crocodile	3–6 years
Dog	1 year	Blue whale	4 years
Songbird	1 year	Camel	4 years
Cattle	1,5–2 years	Harbour or Common seal	4 years
Bat	1–2 years	Carp	4–5 years
Chicken	1–2 years	Baboon	4–8 years
Duck	1–2 years	Lobster	5 years
Sheep	1–2 years	Giraffe	6–7 years
Shrew	1–2 years	Gorilla (female)	6–7 years
Hedgehog	2 years	Chimpanzee	8–10 years
Mole	2 years	Gibbon	8–10 years
Hippopotamus	2,5 years	Gorilla (male)	9–10 years
Hyaena	2–3 years	Dolphin	10–16 years
Lizard	2–3 years	Elephant	12–15 years
Snail	2–3 years	Human	12–18 years
Trout	2–4 years	Rhinoceros	20 years

Planning a family

The speckled padloper is a tiny tortoise, only 7 cm long. That does not stop the female from laying an egg that is 3 cm long or 40% of her body size. (New Zealand's kiwi lays an egg that is 25% of its body size.)

Female killer whales give birth to a calf that weighs 180 kg and is 2,5 m long , which enters the world tail first. The orca is not overly keen on this process, and will only have one offspring every 10 years.

Tilapia mothers have a very good hiding place for their youngsters when there is potential danger. She just opens her mouth and keeps her little fishes safely hidden away until the danger has passed.

First there are two rats. If they should happen to be a male and a female, their union could literally be blessed by one million offspring, all within 18 months of the honeymoon.

Some healthy competition

Young elephant bulls respect their elders, especially when it is mating season. At this time the mature bulls are in a state known as musth (or must), which means that they secrete a smelly brown liquid from a gland between the eye and ear. This is a clear 'come hither' signal to the cows of the herd. At the same time, bulls that are not ready for parenthood secrete a honey-like liquid to let the elder statesmen know that there is no competition for the attention of the females. Not yet, anyway ...

Trunk call

The elephant's trunk can be as long as 1,5 m and weigh as much as 135 kg. The trunk is so strong that an elephant can use it to pick up objects weighing as much as 275 kg, or to push over large trees. The trunk contains 16 large muscles and 150 000 groups of smaller muscles, but there is not a single bone in this interesting appendage. (By comparison, a human's body has a total of 639 muscles.) The trunk ends in two very sensitive tips which can be used to pick up a small blade of grass. The elephant can even pick up a coin from a flat surface with these tips, or break open a peanut shell.

DID YOU KNOW?

◆ *A whale calf is born tail first.*

◆ *The most prolific mammal is the vole. The female can have her first litter of between four and nine little voles when she is just 15 days old. She may have as many as 33 litters in her lifetime.*

Gestation – the long and short of it

Gestation is the time between fertilization and birth. The shortest gestation period known is 12 to 13 days, shared by three marsupials whose young are born while they are still underdeveloped and have to complete their development in the mother's pouch. The longest gestation period for any mammal is that of the African elephant – the cow carries the foetus an average of 660 days, and a maximum of 760 days.

GESTATION PERIODS OF SOME MAMMALS

Mammal	Days	Mammal	Days
Mouse (domestic white)	19	Sheep (domestic)	144–151
Mouse (meadow)	21	Goat (domestic)	145–155
Hedgehog	30	Monkey (rhesus)	164
Rabbit (domestic)	30–35	Baboon	187
Mole	35	Aardvark	210
Grey squirrel	30–40	Hippopotamus	225–250
Cat (domestic)	58–65	Otter	270–300
Dog (domestic)	58–70	Cow	279–292
Guinea pig	68	Seal	330
Warthog	72	Horse	330–342
African wild dog	72	Dolphin	350
Leopard	92–95	Ass	365
Cheetah	95	Zebra (Grant's)	365
Hyaena	93	Giraffe	420–450
Lion	108	Rhinoceros (black)	450
Porcupine	112	Whale (sperm)	480–500
Pig (domestic)	112–115	Elephant	660

It's a shrew's life

The shortest land mammal is Savi's white-toothed pygmy shrew, also known as the Etruscan shrew (*Suncus etruscus*), which lives on the Mediterranean coast and southwards to the Western Cape in South Africa. Its head and body is 36 to 52 mm long, it has a tail of 24 to 29 mm and weighs just 1,5 to 2,5 g.

This tiny shrew has to eat at least every two hours, and it can eat up to three times its own weight every day. That would be equal to a human diet of one sheep, 50 chickens, 60 loaves of bread and about 150 apples – all in one day!

A shrew doesn't have a long life, compared to other mammals. In the wild it will live about 18 months, and in captivity it will last just more than two years.

Some shrews have poisonous saliva. When they bite other small animals, the poison will paralyze their prey.

A family outing

When a family of shrews (which can be quite large) goes out in the wide world, each will hold onto the one in front.

A hero – with a super spine!

The hero shrew has a super-strong spine, with extra joints for flexibility. The size, shape and articulation of the lumbar region differ a lot from those of other insectivores.

It means that this small mammal will be able to withstand the pressure of a human weighing 80 kg standing on its back.

Each vertebra between the animal's rib cage and hips is a corrugated cylinder, and the spine has a series of interlocking parts that articulate with the previous and succeeding vertebrae.

The mass of the spine accounts for nearly 4% of the hero shrew's body weight. This figure is between 0,5 and 1,6% for other small mammals.

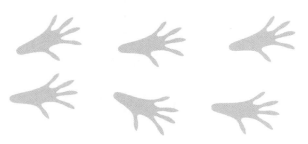

A little greased lightning

The elephant shrew is an alert little fellow and when he scampers away at the slightest sign of danger, he moves like greased lightning! His forelegs are shorter than his back legs and he rushes across the ground with short jumps or hastens about on all 4 legs. In an emergency he can move along at 25 km/h.

A tiny buck

The smallest antelope is western Africa's tiny royal antelope, which is about the size of a hare, standing 25 to 31 cm tall at the shoulder and weighing between 3 and 3,6 kg.

Some interesting animals

Marking territory

A tenrec from Madagascar has quite a ritual to make its presence felt. It marks its territory with the smell of its body. If it wants to mark a place it spits, rubs its paws on its sides to pick up the scent and then rubs its paws in the spit.

Ring-tailed lemurs rub their bottoms on trees as they travel through the forest, leaving a trail for the rest of the troupe.

Hop-along

Madagascar's sifaka has extremely long legs. In fact, its legs are so long that running on all fours is impossible. They move by hopping forward at speed, bouncing from one foot to the other and holding their arms in the air. They don't use this method of travel very often, because they spend most of their time in treetops.

Fossa – the jigsaw puzzle

A fossa is a fairly jumbled animal that lives only in Madagascar – it has a nose like a dog, teeth like a leopard and whiskers like an otter. Although it is as big as a fox, it is the largest predator in Madagascar. Fossas jump from tree to tree in pursuit of lemurs, frogs and lizards.

Browsing high

The gerenuk is an antelope with a small head and large eyes and ears. It stands on its hind legs, and stretches its long neck to reach tall bushes that are as high as 2,5 m from the ground. It even uses its front legs to pull down higher branches.

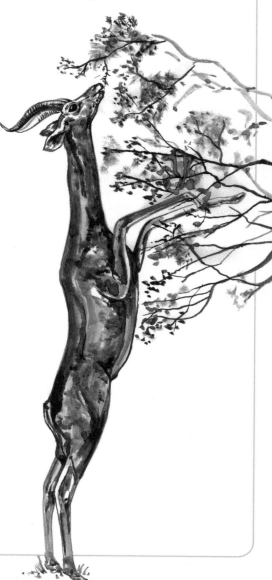

DID YOU KNOW?

- The gerenuk has a special muscle on its lip that is puncture-proof.
- The name 'gerenuk' means 'giraffe-necked' in the Somali language.

Fun facts

- Giraffe can close their nostrils when they run – to keep out dust.
- African pottos can move their thumbs across the palms of their 'hands'. They have a very short first finger, which gives them a very good grip.
- Madagascar's sportive lemur has this name because it puts up its fists like a boxer when it is attacked, and even begins to punch its enemy.
- The addax is an antelope that never drinks water. It gets all the moisture it needs from the plants it eats. That is why it is able to survive in the Sahara Desert.
- Bat-eared foxes like to feast on termites. Their hearing is so well developed that they can even hear termites that are moving underground.

Froggy fun!

- The world's largest frog, the goliath frog, is found in fast-flowing rivers in Cameroon and Equatorial Guinea. Its average length is 30 cm, and its outstretched body can be as long as 75 cm. A specimen that was captured in 1889 on the Sanaga River in Cameroon was 36,8 cm long (87,6 cm with its legs extended), and weighed 3,6 kg. It is entirely mute, because it does not have a vocal bag.
- A male frog found in the Seychelles carries its young around on its back until they become adults.
- The adult pygmy piping frog of the Seychelles is one of the world's smallest frogs – about the size of a large ant.
- The African grey tree-frog builds a foam nest to protect its young from drying up in the heat.
- The clawed frog, found in southern and eastern Africa, spends most of its life in the water and uses its clawed toes to stir up the mud at the bottom of a pond when it is looking for food.
- The male hairy frog of West Africa has a covering of 'hair' on its hind limbs during the breeding season. On closer inspection the hairs are actually tiny skin filaments, with a rich supply of blood vessels. It is believed that they could be respiratory aids that absorb oxygen directly from the water to supplement the oxygen taken in by the frog's poorly developed lungs.
- Biologists have discovered 106 new frogs during a four-year-long survey in the rainforests of eastern Madagascar.
- South Africa has one of the world's most varied frog populations, with more than 50 of its 106 species found nowhere else.

A few bird facts

- A secretary bird walks long distances in search of food. It can cover as much as 24 km in a single day.
- Egyptian vultures have found a creative way to crack open ostrich eggs – they drop rocks on the large eggs. Smaller eggs, also regarded as a delicacy, are opened by dropping the egg on a rock.
- The lanner falcon kills its prey by colliding with it, sometimes with such force that the prey dies instantly.
- A sparrowhawk can turn upside down in mid air to catch its prey.
- The African pygmy falcon is Africa's smallest bird of prey. It is only 19 or 20 cm long, and can weigh as little as 60 g.

A record bird

The largest living bird is the ostrich (*Struthio camelus*), a flightless bird that reaches a height of 2,75 m and weighs up to 156,5 kg. The ostrich is the fastest bird on land, and can reach a swift 72 km/h if necessary, in spite of the fact that it has only two toes on each foot.

The ostrich is a record bird – in all aspects. It is the largest existing bird; it stands taller than any other bird; it is also heavier, runs faster, has a longer neck and longer legs, and the female lays bigger eggs than any other bird. One ostrich egg is equal to the contents of 24 hen's eggs.

DID YOU KNOW?

- The human eye's diameter is 2,4 cm, and a golf ball has a diameter of 4,267 mm.
- The extinct elephant bird of Madagascar laid eggs that weighed 12 kg each.
- An average ostrich egg, which is the equivalent of about 24 hen's eggs, weighs about 1,5 kg.

Ostrich records

- Heaviest living bird
- Tallest living bird
- Longest legs in relation to its body
- Biggest eye of any land animal
- Fastest running bird
- Lays biggest egg
- And heaviest egg
- Smallest egg in relation to body mass
- Biggest eye

Fishy fashions – largest fish

- The world's largest cartilaginous fish is the whale shark, which is found in the warmer parts of the Atlantic and Indian oceans.
- This giant feeds on plankton; it can be as long as 15 m and can weigh up to 18 tons.
- The largest whale shark recorded, caught in 1949, was 12,65 m long, measured 7 m around the thickest part of its body and weighed between 15 and 20 tons.

DID YOU KNOW?

A whale shark egg, found in 1953, measured 30,5 by 9 cm and contained a live embryo that was 35 cm long.

Largest bony fish

- The ocean sunfish, or mola, is the world's largest bony fish, with an average body length of 1,8 m and a length of 2,4 m from the tip of the dorsal fin to the tip of the anal fin.
- It can weigh an impressive 1 ton. The record mola was 3,1 m wide and 4,26 m long, and weighed 2 235 kg.
- This giant ocean sunfish wants to make sure that it leaves a few of its offspring behind. A 1,4 m female's ovary can contain as many as 300 million eggs – the most of any vertebrate. When the small mola hatches, it is only 1,8 mm long.

DID YOU KNOW?

- *The name mola comes from the Latin word for 'millstone' – presumably because of the round shape of the fish.*
- *The mola is known as the sunfish, or even 'schwimmender Kopf' in German, which means 'swimming head'.*
- *The mola is not exactly a brainy fish. Its brain is the size of a walnut and weighs only a few grams.*

Anything dad can do ...

- Lake Tanganyika's mouth-brooding cichlid, a small tropical freshwater fish, produces seven eggs or fewer during normal reproduction.
- When an egg is laid, the female takes it into her mouth, where the male fertilizes it. It is incubated for up to 30 days.

Most venomous fish

The most venomous fish is the reef stonefish, which has 13 poisonous spines on its dorsal fin. A stab from one of these spines is enough to kill a human.

DID YOU KNOW?

One proud Caribbean sea horse father is on record as having given birth to 1 500 offspring.

The slo-o-west swimmer

The sea horse, of which there are about 30 species, is the slowest-moving of all fish. Some smaller species, such as the dwarf sea horse, fairly crawl along at speeds of less than 0,00161 km/h.

Daddy day-care

- The tiny sea horse looks like the knight from a chess board. It has a horse-like face and a body that is protected by rings of bony plates.
- It has vivid skin colours that help it to blend in with its equally colourful surroundings, and it uses its long, curly tail to anchor its body to sea grass.
- When it does move, it swims very slowly and upright.
- The sea horse moves too slowly to chase its food. That is why it will rather ambush its prey, sucking it up with its long tube-like snout.
- A male sea horse cannot be accused of not taking its role as parent seriously. When the time comes for reproduction, the female will position her ovipositor (a long tube) so that the eggs can move to a pouch in the male's body.
- The male fertilizes the eggs, and the little sea horses develop in his body. A few weeks later he will go into 'labour' and produce a multitude of babies, anything from a few dozen to 100.

The fastest fish

The fastest fish over short distances is believed to be the cosmopolitan sailfish. According to a series of speed trials at the Long Key Fishing Camp, Florida, USA, a sailfish took out 91 m of fishing line in three seconds – equivalent to a speed of 109 km/h.

The largest predatory fish

The great white shark has an average length of between 4,3 and 4,6 m, and weighs from 520 to 770 kg. It is believed that the 'white death', as it is known, can grow to lengths of more than 6 m.

This intimidating fish is known by several names: great white shark, death shark, man-eater, tommy, uptail or white pointer.

Food facts

- When does green become pink? When it is eaten by flamingos. Pink is not the flamingo's natural colour, but its favourite food is tiny green algae which turn pink during the digestive process.
- Shrimp have the same effect on the flamingo's colour scheme.
- If people in East Africa are bitten by mosquitoes, they can expect some form of revenge, even if it is not of the instant variety, but happens in a rather roundabout way. Some spiders in this part of the world enjoy devouring the blood-sucking mosquitoes that torment humans.
- Chimpanzees in Tanzania and the Ivory Coast don't care about their cholesterol levels. In fact, they love to eat the fattiest parts of their prey – usually colobus monkeys – first. They will start with the brain, move to the marrow in the long bones and only then do they eat the meat.
- Chimpanzees prefer to eat fruit, leaves and bark with high levels of glucose, sucrose and fructose. Call it the dessert after the main course of saturated fat. Interestingly, chimpanzees are the human's closest relative.
- The elephant is one of the big eaters in nature. It can eat between 100 and 300 kg of food a day, and will guzzle an impressive 190 litres of water as well.
- A swarm of locusts can devour more than 20 000 tons of wheat in a single day.
- The female flea is a bloodthirsty little insect. She can consume 15 times her body weight in blood every day.
- A mole can eat its own weight in earthworms per day.
- Cats can't taste sweet. That's why the big cats just love meat for both their main course and for dessert.
- The theobromine in chocolate can kill a dog.

More proverbs from Africa ...

'The beak of the bird is what tells us the things it eats.' Kaonde
'We will water the thorn for the sake of the rose.' Kanem
'By coming and going, a bird weaves its nest.' Ashanti, Ghana
'One who is crazy for meat hunts buffalo.' Luganda, Uganda
'Every stream has its source.' Zulu
'Who guards two termite hills, returns empty handed.' Bahaya
'If you chase away an ant, all the ants will come and bite you.' Pygmy

DID YOU KNOW?

- *The nautilus shell is a natural example of a logarithmic spiral, where the size of the spiral increases, but its shape is unaltered with each successive curve.*
- *Nautilus comes from a Greek word that means 'sailor'.*

The nautilus

A nautilus is a cephalopod with a squid-like shell that is filled with gas to help it drift in the ocean.

The nautilus lives in the outer chamber of the coiled shell, and as it grows it adds new buoyancy chambers to the shell.

When the nautilus withdraws into its shell, it closes its shell opening with two specially folded tentacles that form a leathery hood.

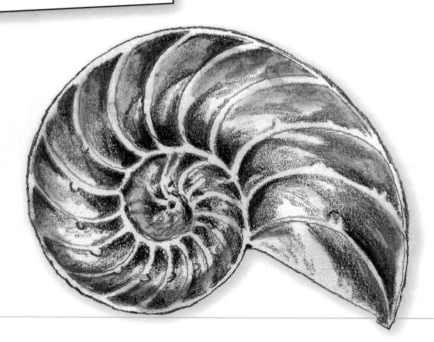

The sunflower

The sunflower's head is a composite flower that consists of many flowers or florets. The outer florets (called ray florets) are sterile and can have a variety of colours besides the well-known yellow – like maroon and orange. The disc florets inside the head grow into seeds, the fruit of the plant.

The florets are arranged in a definite pattern of interconnecting spirals, where the number of left spirals and the number of right spirals are successive Fibonacci numbers. (A Fibonacci sequence is an unending series of numbers in which each number, except for the first two, is the sum of the preceding two. This sequence is quite common in nature). There are 34 spirals in one direction and 55 spirals in the other, but a very large sunflower has 89 spirals in one direction and 144 in the other.

In the bud stage the sunflower is heliotropic, which means that it will follow the sun. When the sun rises, it faces east and during the day it follows the sun so that at sunset it will be facing west. During the night the head turns back, so that it will be facing east again when the sun rises. In the blooming stage sunflowers do not follow the sun anymore, and the stem stays in an eastward orientation.

DID YOU KNOW?
The sunflower is the symbol of the Vegan Society.

The ocean boarder

Hermit crabs are permanent boarders in empty shells discarded by other sea creatures. When they grow too big for their borrowed shells, they leave them in search of new shells.

A giant clam

The giant clam easily lives up to its name. These molluscs can grow to a size of more than 1,2 m across, and weigh as much as 300 kg. That's about three times more than the average rugby player.

The bee's wing-beats

- A worker bee's wings beat between 240 and 250 times per second.
- The soldier bee is even more frenetic, with 285 wing-beats per second.
- The drone is positively lazy, going at a rate of only 207 beats per second in pursuit of the queen, who fairly speeds along at up to 253 beats per second.

More insect wings?

- The dragonfly is a fast flier (30 km/h) but its wings beat only between 22 and 28 times per second.
- The horsefly will buzz along at 96 beats per second, much slower than the housefly (180 to 330 beats per second).
- The record holder for wing-beats per second is the midge, which flaps its tiny wings up to 1 046 times per second.
- And the mosquito? Its annoying buzz is created by between 287 and 307 wing-beats per second.

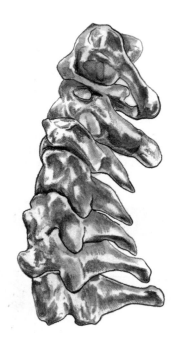

A pain in the neck?

Almost all mammals have seven cervical or neck vertebrae – from the tiny shrew to the tall giraffe and the enormous blue whale. The exceptions are the three-toed sloth (9), Hoffmann's two-toed sloth (6) and the manatee (6).

Amphibians have only one vertebra in their necks, while the crocodile has only two. The turtle will have eight vertebrae in its neck, and a bird's neck will contain 14. The exceptions are the carrion crow with 10, the albatross (15), flamingo (19) and mute swan (26).

More vertebrae

- Humans have 34 vertebrae in their spines. That's the same number as turtles, and only one less than songbirds (35).
- The swan has a total of 56 cervical vertebrae.
- A snake's skeleton consists almost exclusively of vertebrae and ribs, with the boa boasting a total of more than 435 vertebrae.
- A species that can't be called spineless by any stretch of the imagination is the shark, which could have more than 400 vertebrae.

The normal human body temperature is 97,4 °C. How does that compare to the temperature of some other animals?

Name	Temperature
Fish (Sockeye salmon)	5–17°C
Hedgehog (hibernating)	6°C
Fish (Rainbow trout)	12–18°C
Lizard	31–35°C
Bat	31°C
Hedgehog (awake)	35°C
Hippopotamus	35,4°C
Human	36,2–37,8°C
Whale	36,5°C
Ostrich	37,4°C
Dromedary	38,1°C
Dog	38,3–39,0°C
Grasshopper	38,6–42,2°C
Cat	38,8–39°C
Pig	39°C
Sheep	39,5°C
Pigeon	41°C
Chicken	41,5°C
Shrew	43°C

Are they ALL family?

- The rose family is not only famous for its flowering plants, but it also includes well-known (and delicious) fruit like the apple, pear, plum, cherry, almond, apricot, peach, nectarine, loquat and quince.
- The blackberry, dewberry and loganberry belong to a genus of the rose family that includes the raspberry and strawberry.
- Ornamental flowers, such as cinquefoil, hawthorn, spiraea, cotoneaster, firethorn, flowering cherry, flowering quince and rowan, also belong to the rose family.
- Lily is the common name for the family *Liliaceae*, which includes many ornamental lilies, as well as onions and shallots, garlic, chives and leeks – and asparagus, the aloe, water hyacinth, sisal hemp and true hemp, carrion flower, greenbrier yam and sweet potato.

The happy hippo

The hippopotamus has a very broad mouth, with impressive and dangerous long, hooked canines and giant, straight incisors in its lower jaw. Its canines usually grow to a length of 60 cm, but the record length is 1,6383 m! It may be a grass eater, but it can open its mouth to a width of 1,2 m.

When the hippo is submerged its heart slows from 90 beats a minute to 20, so that it can remain underwater longer. A reflex movement activates strong muscles that close its eyes and nose, and when it rises again above the surface it blows the remaining air out of its lungs, making a loud noise.

Many people think that the hippo sweats blood, but the pinkish fluid that can sometimes be seen on its body isn't blood. The hippopotamus does not have sweat glands or fat glands. It has unique glands that exude a red pigment, which cools the animal down and protects it against sunburn and infections. It also uses water and mud to cool down.

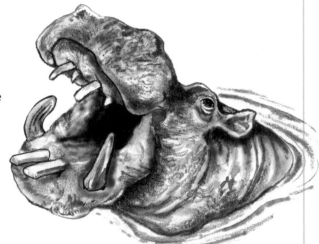

The hippopotamus is surprisingly fast in the water and although it does not look like a great runner on land, it can race along at speeds of up to 48 km/h – much faster than any human athlete!

Cape Town's unique floral paradise

- On 1 July 2004 the World Heritage Committee recognized the Cape Floral Region Protected Areas as South Africa's sixth World Heritage Site.
- The Cape Floral Region Protected Areas cover more than 553 000 ha and include eight separate areas, in a crescent-shaped band from Nieuwoudtville in the north to Cape Town in the south, and then east to Grahamstown.
- It is the world's smallest yet richest floral kingdom, with the highest known concentration of plant species: 1 300 per 10 000 km^2. (The concentration in the South American rain forests, second on this list, is a mere 400 per 10 000 km^2.)
- The Kirstenbosch National Botanical Garden forms part of this site. No other natural World Heritage Site includes a botanical garden.
- It is one of the richest areas for plants in the world, and although it represents less than 0,5% of Africa's total land area, it is home to nearly 20% of the continent's flora. Most of the continent's ecological and biological processes are associated with fynbos vegetation, which is unique to this region.

CAN YOU BELIEVE IT?

◆ *About 75% of South Africa's rare and threatened plants are found in the fynbos biome.*

◆ *The number of species per genus in this region (9:1) and the number of species per family (52) are among the highest for species-rich regions in the world.*

◆ *At least 70% of the 9 600 plant species of the Cape Floral Kingdom are found nowhere else on earth.*

◆ *The species density in the Cape Floral Region is among the highest in the world, and displays the highest levels of endemism (31,9%).*

◆ *Fynbos contains more than a 5% cover of Cape reeds, as well as proteas, ericas and seven plant families found nowhere else in the world. The word 'fynbos' comes from a Dutch word for plants with fine leaves.*

◆ *Of the more than 7 700 fynbos plant species, 70% are endemic to the area. There are more than 600 different species of ericas (heaths) in this area – and only 26 species in the rest of the world.*

◆ *A remarkable feature of fynbos is the number of species that are found in small areas. The total world range of some species can grow in an area smaller than half a rugby field!*

◆ *The Cape Peninsula, including Table Mountain, has an area of only 470 km^2 (as big as London), but it is home to 2 285 different plant species. There are more plant species in this small area than in the whole of Great Britain, which is 5 000 times bigger. Table Mountain alone (57 km^2) supports 1 470 species.*

◆ *The Cape Flats has the world's highest concentration of endangered species in the world – a total of 15 species per km^2 are in danger of extinction. This area of 1 874 km^2 houses more than 1 466 species (of which 76 are found only here).*

South Africa has an estimated 5,8% of the world's total mammal species, 8% of bird species, 4,6% of the global diversity of reptile species, 16% of the total number of marine fish species, and 5,5% of the world's classified insect species.

The running machine

The cheetah's entire body is built for speed, enabling this supreme sprinter to accelerate from 0 to 70 km/h in two seconds. Its top speed is believed to be 112 km/h.

DID YOU KNOW?

In February 1999 a South African cheetah called Nyana Spier was officially timed running 100 m in a record of 6,08 seconds, accelerating from 0 to 80 km/h in 3,6 seconds.

Don't blink!

Four of the fastest land mammals are found in Africa. The cheetah is the fastest, and can reach a speed of more than 100 km/h over a short distance. The blue wildebeest and black wildebeest, lion and Thomson's gazelle can run approximately 80 km/h.

The ultimate sprinter

- The cheetah's body is long and slender, and its skeleton consists of small, light bones. The spine is very flexible and can move up and down, almost like a whip.
- It has muscular hind legs, which enables it to move 7 to 8 m in a single stride.
- The cheetah's small clavicles and shoulder blades help to extend the length of a stride. When it is running, its whole body is entirely airborne for a large part of the time!
- The cheetah's small, aerodynamic head has round ears and large nostrils, so that it can breathe in huge gulps of air to fill its big lungs as fast as possible.
- The legs are lean, long and muscular and its claws, that can be only partially retracted, provide traction – just like spiked track shoes.
- The liver, heart and adrenaline glands are large and provide an explosive force that enables the cheetah to get off the mark very quickly.
- The long, thick tail acts as a rudder, and the cheetah uses it to make an almost instantaneous turn-about.
- There are some disadvantages to the cheetah's build. It can only maintain its speed for about 200 to 300 m – or less than a minute. If it should run slightly less hell for leather, averaging, say 72 km/h, it could go further – as far as 3 km.

DID YOU KNOW?

♦ *When the cheetah is resting, its heart beats 120 to 170 times a minute, and it breathes 20 to 30 times a minute.*

♦ *After a top-speed chase, its heart rate increases to between 200 and 259 beats a minute and it breathes between 150 and 200 times per minute.*

That roach can move!

Some large tropical cockroaches can fairly blitz through a room – at a speed of 5,4 km/h, which works out at about 50 body lengths per second. If the human world record holder in the 100 m could run that fast, he would improve the current world record for the 100 m (9,77 seconds) to a staggering 1,1 seconds!

More speedsters – by sea and air

● The killer whale or orca is the marine mammal that can achieve the fastest swimming speed. It has been recorded swimming at speeds of 55,5 km/h.

● The fastest flying mammal is the big brown bat, which has been recorded at a speed of 25 km/h.

The speedy snail

● The common garden snail is the fastest-moving land snail. The snail that did its species proud even had a name – it was dubbed Verne.

● On 20 February 1990 Verne took part in a 31 cm race (!) at West Middle School in Plymouth, Michigan, USA.

● Verne was triumphant in a record time of 02h13, setting a blistering pace of 0,23 cm/sec. Verne will not threaten any world speed records soon. It will take him about eight days to complete 1,6 km (four laps around an athletic track).

ANIMAL SPEEDS

Crawling, running	Speed		
Edible snail	0,0032 km/h	Human (flying start)	44,6 km/h
Millipede	0,013 km/h	Hippopotamus	48 km/h
Giant tortoise	0,33 km/h	House cat	48 km/h
Centipede	1 km/h	Dromedary	50 km/h
Spider	1,3 km/h	Giraffe	51 km/h
Mole	4 km/h	Rhinoceros	51 km/h
Herbivorous dinosaur	6 km/h	Gnu	60 km/h
Rat	9,6 km/h	Wild horse	60 km/h
Eastern green mamba	11,3 km/h	Wolf	60 km/h
Common house mouse	12 km/h	Hare	65 km/h
Horse (trot)	13,5 km/h	Wild ass	65 km/h
Camel	15 km/h	Zebra	65 km/h
Black mamba	17,6 km/h	Racehorse	69 km/h
Horse (gallop)	36 km/h	Antelope	70 km/h
Human (100 m race)	36,96 km/h	Ostrich	72 km/h
African elephant	39 km/h	Gazelle	75 km/h
		Lion	75 km/h
		Cheetah	112 km/h

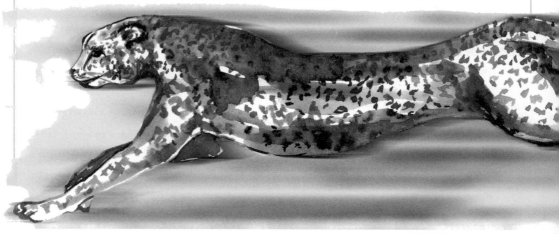

Swimming	Speed
Starfish	0,0006 km/h
Sea snake	3,6 km/h
Human (100 m freestyle)	7 km/h
Grey whale	7,5 km/h
Eel	12 km/h
Trout	35 km/h
Gentoo penguin (under water)	36 km/h
Shark	36 km/h
Salmon	39 km/h
Giant squid	40 km/h
Dolphin	46 km/h
Fin whale	55 km/h
Orca	65 km/h
Tuna	75 km/h
Marlin	80 km/h
Swordfish	90 km/h

Flying	Speed
Mosquito	1,4 km/h
Housefly	8,2 km/h
Blowfly	11 km/h
Small white (butterfly)	14 km/h
Migratory locust	16 km/h
Bumblebee	18 km/h
Bee	29 km/h
Dragonfly	30 km/h
Common buzzard	45 km/h
House sparrow	45 km/h
Stork	45 km/h
Bat	50 km/h
Horsefly	50 km/h
Swan	50 km/h
Crows	59 km/h
Small passerine	61 km/h
Swallow	65 km/h
Albatross	70 km/h
Flying fish	75 km/h
Falcon	79 km/h
European starling	81 km/h
Goose	91 km/h
Common swift	180 km/h
Peregrine falcon (swooping)	290 km/h

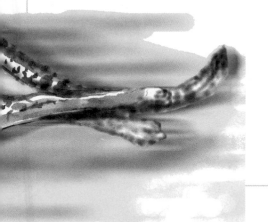

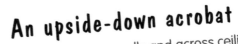

An upside-down acrobat

The gecko can run up walls and across ceilings thanks to soft, brush-like pads on the bottom of their feet. The pads consist of millions of minute bristles that will hook in any cracks on uneven surfaces.

Under the sea – fun facts

- Limpets spend the day creeping over rocks, scraping up tiny bits of food with their tongues. They return to the same place on the rocks every night – but no one knows how they find it.

- A mussel's 'beard' is very useful – it is actually a very strong, fine thread that sticks to almost anything, and gives it a very firm grip on a rock.

- Sea anemones may look like wild flowers, but they are actually meat-eating animals. They are close cousins of the jellyfish – but instead of floating around, they stay in one place and trap smaller creatures in their stinging tentacles.

- Sea urchins may look like balls of spikes, but they actually have rows of flexible tubular feet hidden among their prickly spines. They have mouths on their undersides, with five strong teeth. They creep along on their flexible feet, their mouths to the sea floor, munching on tiny plants and animals.

The urban life – insect style

Tropical termites should be used to urban life – they live in colonies with a population of more than three million.

Honeybees like company and a hive can contain between 40 000 and 80 000 bees with different occupations.

AFRICA'S NATIONAL BIRDS

Angola	Peregrine falcon	*Falco peregrinus*
Botswana	Lilac-breasted roller or Cattle egret	*Coracias caudatus* or *Bubulcus ibis*
Kenya	Rooster or Black crowned crane (both unofficial)	*Gallus gallus* or *Balearica pavonina*
Lesotho	Southern bald ibis	*Geronticus calvus*
Liberia	Common bulbul	*Pycnonotus barbatus*
Malawi	Bar-tailed trogon	*Apaloderma vittatum*
Mauritius	Dodo	*Raphus cucullatus*
Namibia	Crimson-breasted shrike	*Laniarius atrococcineus*
Nigeria	Black crowned crane	*Balearica pavonina*
Rwanda	Grey crowned crane (unofficial)	*Balearica regulorum*
São Tomé and Príncipe	African grey parrot and Black kite	*Psittacus erithacus* and *Milvus migrans*
Seychelles	Seychelles black parrot	*Coracopsis nigra barklyi*
South Africa	Blue crane	*Anthropoides paradisea*
Sudan	Secretary bird	*Sagittarius serpentarius*
Swaziland	Purple-crested turaco	*Gallirex porphyreolophus tauraco*
Tanzania	Grey crowned crane (unofficial)	*Balearica regulorum*
Uganda	Grey crowned crane	*Balearica regulorum*
Zambia	African fish eagle	*Haliaeetus vocifer*
Zimbabwe	African fish eagle	*Haliaeetus vocifer*

Keratin

A bird's feathers are made from keratin, the same protein that is found in hair, nails and rhinoceros horn. The scales on a lizard's skin also consist of keratin.

A powerful stink

A skunk's stink is quite powerful – you can smell it from a distance of 300 m.

How old?

Scientists use the plugs in a dolphin's ears to determine its age. The plugs consist of layers of keratin that grow constantly.

Some scales

Pangolins or scaly anteaters are the only mammals with scales, which are formed from hairs that are tightly joined together. When it is attacked, the pangolin will raise the scales with its sharp edges.

One hump or two?

- About 90% of the world's camels are dromedaries, also called the Arabian camel. This species is totally domesticated.
- The dromedary is the camel with one hump, while the Bactrian camel has two humps. Camels use the humps to store fat, not water.
- A camel can go for nine days without water and 33 days without food. The hump stores fat that can be used for energy when there is no food.
- The hump of a healthy, well-fed camel may weigh 35 kg or more. The size of the hump depends on the amount of fat in it. When food is scarce, the hump is smaller. A camel can last a week or more without water, but it can survive several months without food.
- When it does get an opportunity to drink water, it could guzzle as much as 100 litres of water in just 10 minutes. That's about two-thirds of a bathtub full of water.
- It can even drink brackish or salt water without getting sick.
- Camels are well adapted for a life in the desert. A thin, clear membrane on each eye protects it from the sand during sandstorms, and double rows of extra-long eyelashes help to keep the sand out of its eyes. It can even close its nostrils.
- Its feet are large and broad to keep it from sinking into the sand.
- Glands supply the eyes with a great deal of water to keep them moist, and thick eyebrows shield the eyes from the desert sun.

DID YOU KNOW?

◆ *The camel is not a silent beast of burden. It can moan and groan, emit high-pitched bleats and loud bellows and roars, and its rumbling growl was one of the noises used to create Chewbacca's voice for the Star Wars movies.*

◆ *When a camel feels threatened, it will spit the contents of its stomach at its enemy, along with some saliva.*

◆ *Camels move both legs from the same side of the body at the same time while it is walking, a gait they share with only two other animals – the giraffe and the cat.*

◆ *Camel hair brushes are not made of camel's hair. They were invented by a man named Mr Camel.*

No sweat!

◆ Camels do not pant and they sweat very little.

◆ A healthy camel's body temperature fluctuates throughout the day, varying from 34°C to 41,7°C. This allows the camel to conserve water by not sweating as the temperature rises.

◆ The camel has a unique body thermostat, which can raise its body temperature tolerance level as much as 6°C before perspiring, thus conserving body fluids and avoiding unnecessary water loss.

◆ The normal walking speed for a camel is 5 km/h. Racing camels reach 20 km/h when they gallop. A working camel will cover 40 km a day.

91

The desert survivor

- Addax antelopes are nearly extinct in the wild, with only about 500 remaining in the wild. Probably the only reason they are still alive in the wild at all is the fact that they can live in uninhabitable places with extreme heat, extensive sand dunes, and other harsh conditions where it is extremely difficult for humans and other predators to reach them. Most addaxes can be found in the southwestern parts of the Sahara Desert.
- The addax has broad, flat hoofs with flat soles to prevent them from sinking into the soft desert sand.
- Its coat changes colour to maintain its body temperature. In winter it is dark greyish-brown and in summer it is white.
- To stay away from the scorching sun the addax will dig a depression in the sand, often in the shade of a boulder, where it can rest.
- It is well adapted to the desert environment, and rarely needs to drink water. It gets most of its water from the plants it eats.

A quilly little fellow

Hedgehog quills are not barbed or poisonous, but these prickly little mammals will apply a foamy saliva to their quills. This may act as an irritant to predators and a natural insect repellent.

With the help of a large muscle that runs along its stomach, the hedgehog pulls its body into a tight, spiky little ball to keep itself out of the jaws of a predator.

When a hedgehog is born, the spines are just below the skin, but they start to appear within 24 hours.

Hedgehogs have a high tolerance to natural and human-made toxins and they can eat animals whose toxins could be fatal to humans, including certain beetles, wasps, bees and venomous snakes.

The pronking addra

The addra lives mainly in the Sahara Desert and is the largest gazelle, with very long legs that provide an extra surface area on its body to get rid of heat.

The addra 'pronks' just like the springbok, hopping up and down with all four of its legs stiff so that its limbs all leave and touch the ground at the same time.

A sacred survivor

Certain African tribes regard the ankole as a sacred animal. These animals have strong herding and protection instincts, and at night the adults will stay in a circle, facing outwards, with the calves in the middle.

Ankoles have been domesticated in parts of Africa for thousands of years, and can survive several months without much food or water.

Bongo!

The bongo, the largest forest antelope, was only discovered by biologists in the 1950s. Because local people regard them with superstition, these animals have been largely unharmed in their traditional habitats. Some bongos have been known to eat burnt wood after lightning storms, as a means of getting salt or minerals. Although they are great high jumpers, they prefer to go under or round obstacles.

When they have to find their way through dense forests, bongos will tilt their chins upwards, causing their horns to lie flat against their backs. Some older bongos often have bald spots on their backs – caused by the tips of their horns rubbing away fur.

A whistling kob

The Uganda kob is a medium-sized antelope with a brownish coat, medium-length horns and large ears.

The male marks its territory by whistling. In order to evade a predator, kobs will leap into the air or hide in water or reed beds.

The bombardier beetle

- If an ant or other insect should decide to take on the cold-blooded bombardier beetle, it is in for a nasty surprise. The beetle will live up to its name by delivering a chemical spray as hot as boiling water.

- The beetle has been issued with two identical glands lying side by side at the back of its abdomen, and an opening at the tip of the abdomen. Each gland has an inner chamber containing hydrogen peroxide and hydroquinones, and an outer chamber with catalase and peroxidase.

- The chemicals from the inner chamber are forced through the outer chamber, and when they react, the effect is explosive and quite shocking for the attacker.

- The vapour that is created in this way leaves the abdomen with an audible bang and at a scalding temperature.

- To add insult to injury the bombardier's aim is very precise, and it can rotate its abdomen through 270° in any direction, and shoot over its back to a pair of reflectors that will ricochet the spray at an extra angle.

- The message? Don't mess with the bombardier beetle!

The coconut's name

There is an interesting story about the origin of the generic word 'cocos' that is used for the coconut. When Portuguese and Spanish traders introduced the coconut into West Africa after 1500, they used the name *coco*, a Portuguese or Spanish slang word for 'monkey face', because that is what the eye pattern on the endocarp and the brown, fibrous hair look like.

The benefits of living together

Some species of acacia trees have an interesting relationship with the acacia ant.

These acacias do not have the chemical defence system used by most other acacias, and without these bitter alkaloids, insects and browsers would eat the leaves and branches at will, slowing down growth of the trees.

Acacia ants live inside inflated thorns at the base of leaves, protecting the trees from hungry mammals. The ants also prune away parasitic plants that grow on its host.

The termite farmers

About 200 ant species farm fungi in their nests as a source of food. This is also done by 3 500 species of beetle and 330 termite species. The African termite cultivates a fungus that grows on its faeces and it constructs a whole mound in such a way that the correct temperature – precisely 30,1°C – is always maintained.

This requires painstaking planning and execution. They dig holes to the water table to keep a pit under the nest damp. The main part of the mound, a 1-m-deep cellar with a diameter of 3 m, is supported by a strong pillar.

The temperature in the mound is maintained by condensation veins on the ceiling and ventilation ducts on the walls.

The whole structure has a number of hollow towers that rise up to 6 m into the air.

The pronking springbok

- The springbok is a small antelope, standing about 75 cm high and weighing 40 kg. The ram's horns are thicker and rougher than those of the female.
- Springbok live in large herds in summer, but move around in smaller herds during winter, eating grass and leaves. They get most of their moisture from succulents, wild watermelons and cucumbers, and shallow roots and bulbs that they dig up.
- Springbok can drink water with a mineral content too high for other animals.
- The word *marsupialis* in its Latin name, *Antidorcas marsupialis,* means 'pouch', and refers to the 10 cm pouch or crest that is hidden under two folds of scent-secreting skin on the back and hind parts of the springbok.
- The springbok can unfold this bag or crest, spreading the white bristles in it, and giving off its typical scent. This is often done when it is in a state of excitement, and the display is usually accompanied by leaps.
- These leaps are part of a typical jumping display, known as 'pronking' or 'stotting', which can be described as slow bounces. It can jump as high as 2 to 4 m and as far as 15 m. Other members of the herd will follow the example of the first to pronk.

Birds of a feather

The red-billed quelea is not a solitary bird. On the contrary. These birds can be found in large flocks, some said to contain as many as 32 million birds. Each bird weighs only about 28 g, which means that the weight of a flock would be 896 tons. Because these birds are seed eaters that eat a sixth of their body weight per day, they can destroy farmers' crops in the blink of an eye.

A world traveller

The Arctic tern is a small bird – but boy, can it travel!

On its annual migration trip it will fly from its Arctic breeding grounds to the Antarctic and back again – a distance of between 32 000 and 40 000 km. By doing this, the Arctic tern experiences two summers per year and skips winter altogether. It must love daylight, because that is about all it ever sees.

During its life, the little tern can travel a distance equal to a trip to the moon and back – more than 800 000 km.

DID YOU KNOW?

There are about 1,5 billion queleas in the world, and they need 42 million tons of seeds – every single day!

An Arctic tern chick that was ringed in Canada in July 1928, made its way to South Africa before the end of that year.

HOW LONG DO THEY LIVE?

Invertebrates	
Species	**Lifespan**
Fruit fly	46 days
Housefly	76 days
Worker bee	6 weeks
Common bedbug	6 months
Octopus	2–3 years
Queen bee	5 years
Centipede	5–6 years
Earwig	7 years
Praying mantis	8 years
Earthworm	10 years
Oyster	12 years
Spider	20 years
Crayfish	20–30 years
Termite queen	25–50 years
Tapeworm	35 years

Fish	
Species	**Lifespan**
Sea horse	5 years
Salmon	13 years
Trout	18 years
Goldfish	41 years
Whale shark	70 years
Carp	70–100 years
Eel	88 years

Amphibians	
Species	**Lifespan**
Tree frog	22 years
Common toad	40 years

A few life stories

- A dragonfly has a lifespan of 24 hours.
- A mayfly lives only one day.
- The housefly's complete life cycle takes between 10 and 21 days.
- Worker ants may live seven years and the queen may live as long as 15 years.
- One way to tell the age of a fish is by looking at its scales, which have growth rings just like trees. These rings are known as circuli and clusters of them are called annuli. Each annuli indicates a period of one year.
- Bullfrogs can live 30 years and the African clawed toad can last 15 years.
- The average scorpion probably lives three to five years, but some species live at least 10 to 15 years.
- Queen termites are the longest living insects. They can live for 50 years.
- The rhinoceros generally lives more than 50 years.

Reptiles	
Species	Lifespan
Lizards	5–8 years
Cobra	28 years
Tortoise	150 years

Birds	
Species	Lifespan
Barn owl	14 years
Swallow	16 years
Common swift	21 years
House sparrow	23 years
Canary	24 years
Duck	25 years
Penguin	26 years
Chicken	30 years
Swan	30 years
Goose	31 years
Pigeon/dove	35 years
Cuckoo	40 years
Pelican	50–60 years
Owl	60–70 years
Eagle	60–80 years
Ostrich	62 years
Stork	70–100 years
Crow	118 years

Mammals	
Species	Lifespan
Shrew	1,5 years
Rat	3 years
Mole	3–4 years
Mouse	4 years
Fox	14 years
Hedgehog	14 years
Wolf	14 years
Dog	15–20 years
Rabbit	18 years
Sheep	20 years
Cattle	20–25 years
Dolphin	25–30 years
Domestic pig	27 years
Camel	28–29 years
Lion	30 years
Giraffe	34 years
Baboon	35 years
Cat	35 years
Zebra	38 years
Horse	40–50 years
Rhinoceros	45 years
Chimpanzee	>50 years
Hippotamus	54 years
Hedgehog	60 years
Elephant	70 years
Donkey	100 years
Whale	100 years
Human	118 years

A long, longer, longest life

The animal with the longest lifespan is the slow-moving giant tortoise, which can easily live more than 150 years. It is believed that the British explorer, Captain Cook, presented the Tongan royal family with a Madagascar radiated tortoise in the 1770s. This animal died only in 1965, after a long life, spanning at least 188 years. Several of its Galápagos cousins have lived way past the age of 150 years.

A long life – relatively speaking

- The mammal with the longest lifespan is the human, which may live well over 100 years.
- Whales can also live a long time, and the fin whale is believed to live between 90 and 100 years.
- The oldest land mammal after the human is the elephant which is believed to reach an age of more than 80 years. The highest verified age is 86 years for an Asian elephant bull named Un Wang, who died in 2003 in Taiwan.
- Another aged pachyderm was Modoc, who died in 1975 in California, having reached the ripe old age of 75 years. Modoc was a heroine who saved a number of circus lions when she pulled their cage out of a burning circus tent.
- Other animals with long lifespans are the giant tortoise (more than 150 years) and the deep-sea clam (100 years).

More oldies

◆ The oldest known bat lived to the age of 31 years in the London Zoo. In the wild, these flying mammals will live between 10 and 20 years.

◆ The oldest lion on record was a guest of the Cologne Zoo in Germany, where it entertained visitors for 29 years. Its wild family will live 12 to 14 years.

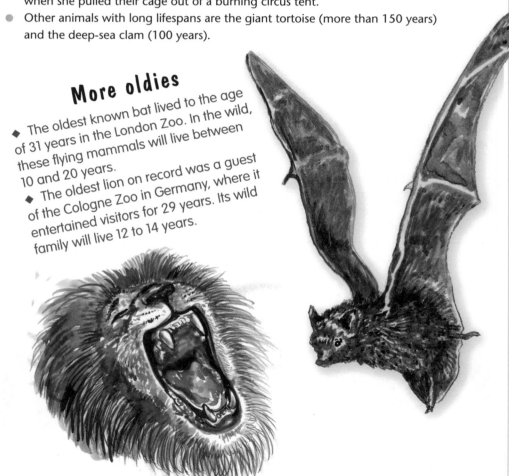

The fear

Not all people are fans of wildlife – some are slightly afraid of any creature outside the house, while others are downright frightened of the animal life and plants that thrive in Africa. An interesting phenomenon is that these fears are named almost as soon as they are identified. Here are a number of the most interesting phobias. And don't worry if you have some of these fears – even some great historical figures had their phobias.

Be afraid – be VERY afraid!

Fear of dogs or rabies is cynophobia, while the fear of cats has various names – ailurophobia, elurophobia, galeophobia, gatophobia or felinophobia.

DID YOU KNOW?

The great Napoleon was one of the world's best-known ailurophobes! As were Adolf Hitler and Alexander the Great.

Those horrid creepy-crawlies

- Some people can't stand the various creepy-crawlies that share the planet with us. The first step to curing a phobia is its correct diagnosis. If these bugs, in whatever disguise they come, still give you goose bumps (which, by the way, is called a **'pilerection'**), it could help to give your fears grand names!
- Maybe you are excessively afraid of itching or insects that could cause itching? Then you could have **acarophobia**. The mere sight of frogs could cause an attack of **ranidaphobia**.
- If you have a morbid dislike of spiders, you suffer from **arachnephobia** (also known as **arachnophobia**).
- Another name for the heebie-jeebies that amphibians, such as frogs, newts and salamanders, give you is **batrachophobia**.
- Fear of worms is **scoleciphobia**, and if it is more specifically the tapeworm that uses your insides as a guest room, you have **taeniophobia**.
- What about a fear of being infested with worms? That is **helminthophobia**. And lice? Easy – just tell your GP you suffer from **pediculophobia** or **phthirophobia**, and he or she will be suitably impressed.

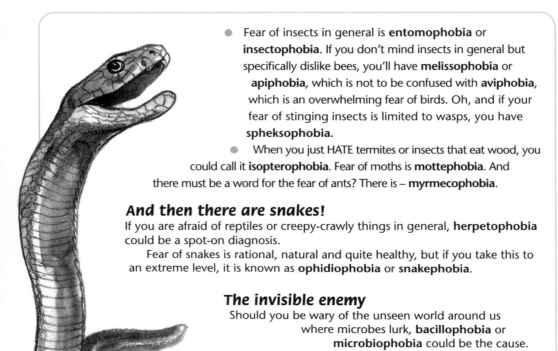

- Fear of insects in general is **entomophobia** or **insectophobia**. If you don't mind insects in general but specifically dislike bees, you'll have **melissophobia** or **apiphobia**, which is not to be confused with **aviphobia**, which is an overwhelming fear of birds. Oh, and if your fear of stinging insects is limited to wasps, you have **spheksophobia**.

- When you just HATE termites or insects that eat wood, you could call it **isopterophobia**. Fear of moths is **mottephobia**. And there must be a word for the fear of ants? There is – **myrmecophobia**.

And then there are snakes!

If you are afraid of reptiles or creepy-crawly things in general, **herpetophobia** could be a spot-on diagnosis.

Fear of snakes is rational, natural and quite healthy, but if you take this to an extreme level, it is known as **ophidiophobia** or **snakephobia**.

The invisible enemy

Should you be wary of the unseen world around us where microbes lurk, **bacillophobia** or **microbiophobia** could be the cause. Your fear of bacteria could spark an attack of **bacteriophobia**, and if your fear is of dirt or germs in general, **mysophobia** or **molysomophobia** will describe your ailment – or **spermatophobia** or **spermophobia** or **verminophobia**. Is it is just dust that frightens you? Call it **amathophobia** or **koniophobia**.

Those horrible birds

If your phobia soars into the realm of birds, **aviphobia** or **ornithophobia** could cover it, but if you are only afraid of being tickled by feathers, you should call it **pteronophobia**. If chickens make you want to scream, you could well have **alektorophobia**.

The scary realms of the animal world

- Maybe it is the bigger animals that scare you spitless. Well, if all animals scare you, you have **zoophobia**, but if they're only wild animals, it will be **agrizoophobia**. If just their skin or fur makes your toes curl, you have **doraphobia**.
- Rabies itself, which is a very serious disease, is known as **hydrophobia**, so the fear of rabies is **hydrophobophobia**, or, alternatively, **kynophobia** or **lyssophobia**.
- Do you have a deep-seated horror of mice? Then you suffer from **musophobia** or **muriphobia** or **suriphobia**. Fortunately the great mole-rat is not that common a sight, but should you have crossed paths with the naked little digger, the resulting affliction could well be **zemmiphobia**.

Little shop of horrors?

- If you have a clear policy of 'people inside, gardens outside', you could contract a number of phobias. Should you hate the sight of flowers, you could name your excuse **anthrophobia** or **anthophobia**, but if this fear should extend to all plants, you will have **botanophobia**.
- Oh, it's only trees that make your heart palpitate? That's easy. You have **dendrophobia**. Should it extend to forests, the correct diagnosis is **hylophobia**.
- Some people have a healthy aversion to vegetables. There is a snazzy name for it – **lachanophobia**. If it is specifically a fear of mushrooms, **mycophobia** is the term, and if garlic makes you break out in a cold sweat, **alliumphobia** will be your reason to avoid it.

Don't go outside!

When you're outside in a thunderstorm, the best advice is: 'Go inside!' If you still have an unhealthy fear of thunder and lightning, even though you are as deep under your bed as you can get, you could suffer from a case of **ceraunophobia**, also known as **keraunophobia**, **astraphobia** or **astrapophobia**. And do you actually dread the thought of a hurricane or tornado ripping the house away from above your bed? Then you have a case of **lilapsophobia**.

BIBLIOGRAPHY

Bailey, Jacqui. *Amazing Animal Facts*. New York: DK Publishing, 2003.

Beyer, Judy (Ed). *Reader's Digest Essential Guide to Southern African Wildlife*. Cape Town: The Reader's Digest Association, South Africa, 2002.

Bonner, John Tyler. *Why Size Matters*. Princeton: Princeton University Press, 2006.

Brown, Augustus. *Why Pandas do Handstands*. London: Bantam Press, 2006.

Carruthers, Vincent (Ed). *Frogs and Frogging in Southern Africa*. Cape Town: Struik, 2001.

Carruthers, Vincent (Ed). *The Wildlife of Southern Africa*. Cape Town: Struik, 2000.

Carwardine, Mark. *Extreme Nature*. London: Harper Collins Publishers Ltd., 2005.

Coyne, Celia et al (Ed). *1000 Wonders of Nature*. London: The Reader's Digest Association, 2001.

Downer, John. *Supersense*. London: BBC Books, 1988.

Flindt, Rainer. *Amazing Numbers in Biology*. Heidelberg: Springer-Verlag, 2006.

Hockey, PAR, et al (Ed). *Roberts Birds of Southern Africa*. VIIth Edition. Cape Town: John Voelcker Bird Book Fund, 2005.

Khan, Sarah. *Amazing Animal Facts and Lists*. London: UsbornePublishing Ltd, 2003.

Marais, Johan. *'n Volledige Gids tot die Slange van Suider-Afrika*. Cape Town: Struik, 2004.

Olwagen, G. (Ed) *Ons Wonderlike Wêreld*. Cape Town: Huisgenoot, nd.

Skinner, John D. & Chimimba, Christian T. (Revised) *The Mammals of the Southern African Subregion*. Cape Town: Cambridge University Press. 2005.

Tison, Annette & Taylor, Talus. *The Animal Book of Records*. London: Macdonald & Co Ltd, 1984.

Van Lill, Dawid. *Amazing Africa*. Pretoria, LAPA Publishers, 2007.

Van Lill, Dawid. *Amazing Animals of Southern Africa*. Pretoria, LAPA Publishers, 2007.

Van Lill, Dawid. *Wonders of Africa*. Pretoria, LAPA Publishers, 2006.

Van Lill, Dawid. *Van Lill's South African Miscellany*. Cape Town: Zebra Press, 2004.

Wootton, Anthony. *Ingenious Insects*. London: J.M. Dent & Sons Ltd, 1983.

WEBSITES

General animaldiversity.ummz.umich.edu/
www.botany.uwc.ac.za/Envfacts/facts/biosa.htm
www.4to40.com/omg/index.asp?id=1340&category=animal
www.africanfauna.com/amazinganimalfacts.php
www.amusingfacts.com/facts/Animals_and_Creatures/
www.bogleech.com/bio-aqua.html
www.centralpets.com/animals/fish/saltwater_inverts/swi1812.html
www.cephbase.utmb.edu/TCP/faq/TCPfaq2b.cfm?ID=37)
www.corsinet.com/trivia/average.html
www.cstone.net/~bcp/4/4JSci.htm
www.ecoworld.com/animals
www.fanoos.com/entertainment/animals_interesting_facts.html
www.funshun.com/amazing-facts/other-animal-facts.html
www.geocities.com/oddfacts1234/
www.g-kexoticfarms.com/did_ya_know.htm
www.interestingfacts.org/?page=category&id=5
www.mbayaq.org/efc/living_species/default.asp?inhab=407
www.mundayweb.com/uselessfacts/animal.php
www.museums.org.za/bio/spiderweb/scytodid.htm
www.planetozkids.com/oban/animals/weird.htm
www.rarespecies.org/kids/feath.htm
www.seaworld.org/animal-info/animal-bytes/
www.strangezoo.com/content/item/113981.html
www.thatsweird.net/facts6.shtml
www.thebeststuffintheworld.com/category/weird-animal
www.triviaplaying.com/02_animal_.htm
www.unexplained-mysteries.com/forum/lofiversion/index.php/t35383.html
www.zilvan.com/funnyfacts/index.htm

Records extremescience.com/index.html
library.thinkquest.org/25014/factsquotes/facts.html
news.nationalgeographic.com/news/2007/01/070116-weird-species_2.html
en.wikipedia.org/wiki/Largest_body_part
whom.co.uk/squelch/incred_creatures.htm
www.enchantedlearning.com/coloring/extremes.shtml

Bat home.earthlink.net/~cmsquare/batfacts.html
library.thinkquest.org/J0112123/bats.htm

www.answers.com/topic/african-long-tongued-fruit-bat

www.batcon.org/home/index.asp?idPage=91

Birds www.birding.com/birdrecords1.asp

Blue whale www.acsonline.org/factpack/bluewhl.htm

Brain fc.units.it/ppb/NeuroBiol/Neuroscienze%20per%2
0tutti/tt.html

www.dls.ym.edu.tw/neuroscience/tt.html

Camel www.sandiegozoo.org/animalbytes/t-camel.html

camelfarm.com/camels/camels_about.html

encarta.msn.com/media_461577461/Camel_Quick_
Facts.html

www.arab.net/camels/

Clawed toad www.interesting.vaty.net/2006/09/
african-clawed-toad.html

Colobus www.britannica.com/eb/
article-9024801/colobus

www.honoluluzoo.org/colobus_monkey.htm

Desert locusts en.wikipedia.org/wiki/Desert_locust

Dog www.thewebsiteofeverything.com/animals/
mammals/Carnivora/Canidae/Lycaon/
Lycaon-pictus.html

Dolphin www.crystalinks.com/dolphin.html

www.everwonder.com/david/dolphins/facts.html

Food www.geocities.com/plecoboy88/fastfood.html

Frog en.wikipedia.org/wiki/African_Foam-nest_Tree_Frog

www.answers.com/topic/xenopus

www.ipcc.ie/worldfrogs.html

Hippo www.funtrivia.com/Animals/Hippos.html

Hyena www.wearesites.com/Personal/Hyenas/
spotted_pics.php

www.wearesites.com/Personal/Hyenas/aardwolf.php

Insect library.thinkquest.org/C0121001/af_insects.htm

Jerboa www.answers.com/topic/jerboa

Killer whale www.thebigzoo.com/
Animals/Killer_Whale.asp

Limpet www.livescience.com/animals/061025_fish_
mouth.html

en.wikipedia.org/wiki/Keyhole_limpet

Longevity www.sjsu.edu/faculty/watkins/longevity.htm

Naked mole-rat nationalzoo.si.edu/Animals/
SmallMammals/fact-nakedmolerat.cfm

Nile crocodile en.wikipedia.org/wiki/Nile_crocodile

www.angelfire.com/mo2/animals1/crocodile/nile.html

Ocean sunfish www.oceansunfish.org/sightings.html

Oceans oceanlink.island.net/oceanmatters/
strandings.html

oceanlink.island.net/records.html

Okapi simple.wikipedia.org/wiki/Okapi

Pangolin en.wikipedia.org/wiki/Pangolin

Pygmy shrew www.answers.com/topic/savi-s-pygmy-shrew

Seal www.oceansafrica.com/seals.htm

Shrimp www.explorebiodiversity.com/Hawaii/
Shrimp-goby/general/Grundel-Krebs.htm

Stick insect news.nationalgeographic.com/
news/2002/03/0328_0328_TVstickinsect.html

Sunflower ttp://en.wikipedia.org/wiki/Sunflower

Teeth news.bbc.co.uk/cbbcnews/hi/find_out/guides/
tech/teeth/newsid_3830000/3830561.stm

www.ais.up.ac.za/vet/dental/dental1.htm

www.ais.up.ac.za/vet/infomania/infomania10/dental10.htm

www.earthlife.net/mammals/teeth.html

Temperatures www.indiana.edu/~animal/fun/
conversions/temperature.html

Turtle www.oceansafrica.com/turtles.htm

Warthog www.yptenc.org.uk/docs/factsheets/animal_
facts/warthog.html

Whale fusionanomaly.net/whales.html

www.cetacea.org/

www.oceansafrica.com/whales.htm

www.vanaqua.org/conserv/Cetacean/Field/field.htm

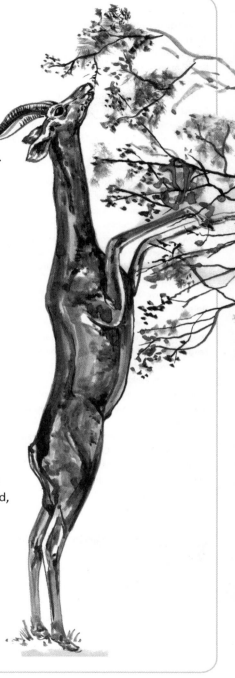

Published by Struik Nature
(an imprint of Random House Struik (Pty) Ltd)
Reg. No. 1966/003153/07
80 McKenzie Street, Cape Town, 8001
PO Box 1144, Cape Town, 8000 South Africa

Visit us at **www.randomstruik.co.za**.
Log on to our photographic website
www.imagesofafrica.co.za for an African experience.

First published 2008
10 9 8 7 6 5 4 3

Copyright © in text, 2008: Dawid van Lill
Copyright © in illustrations, 2008: Dawid van Lill
Copyright © in published edition, 2008:
Random House Struik (Pty) Ltd

Publishing manager: Pippa Parker
Managing editor: Helen de Villiers
Designer: Janice Evans
Editor: Cynthia Kemp
Proofreader: Glynne Newlands
Illustrations: Annelise Meyer
Cover illustrations: Rufus Papenfus

Reproduction by Hirt & Carter Cape (Pty) Ltd
Printed and bound by Paarl Media

All rights reserved. No part of this publication may be
reproduced, stored in a retrieval system, or transmitted,
in any form or by any means, electronic, mechanical,
photocopying, recording or otherwise, without the
prior written permission of the copyright owner(s).

ISBN 978 1 77007 523 8

Also available in Afrikaans as
Natuurtrivia uit Afrika 978 1 77007 522 1